Iguanas in Your Home

A Complete and Up-to-Date Guide

Approved by the A.S.P.C.A.

R.M. Smith

Published in association with T.F.H. Publications, Inc.,
the world's largest and most respected publisher of pet literature

Chelsea House Publishers
Philadelphia

Basic Domestic Pet Library
A Cat in the Family
Amphibians Today
Aquarium Beautiful
Choosing the Perfect Cat
Dog Obedience Training
Dogs: Selecting the Best Dog for You
Ferrets Today
Guppies Today
Hamsters Today
Housebreaking and Training Puppies
Iguanas in Your Home
Kingsnakes & Milk Snakes
Kittens Today
Lovebirds Today
Parakeets Today
Pot-bellied Pigs
Rabbits Today
Turtles Today

Publisher's Note: All of the photographs in this book have been coated with FOTOGLAZE™ finish, a special lamination that imparts a new dimension of colorful gloss to the photographs.

Reinforced Library Binding & Super-Highest Quality Boards

Library of Congress Cataloging-in-Publication Data

Smith, R. M.
    Iguanas in your home : a complete and up-to-date guide / R.M.
Smith.
        p.   cm. -- (Basic domestic pet library)
    "Approved by the A.S.P.C.A."
    Includes index.
    ISBN 0-7910-4611-7 (hardcover)
    1. Iguanas as pets.   I. American Society for the Prevention of
Cruelty to Animals. II. Title. III. Series.
SF459.I38S64 1997
639.3'95--dc21
                                                            97-4184
                                                                CIP

IGUANAS
In Your Home

by R. M. Smith

A QUARTERLY

yearBOOKS,INC.
Dr. Herbert R. Axelrod,
Founder & Chairman
Neal Pronek
Chief Editor
W. P. Mara
Editor

yearBOOKS and Quarter-
lies are all photo com-
posed, color separated, and
designed
on Scitex equipment in
Neptune, N.J. with the
following staff:

DIGITAL PRE-PRESS
Michael L. Secord
Supervisor
Sherise Buhagiar
Patti Escabi
Cynthia Fleureton
Sandra Taylor Gale
Pat Marotta
Joanne Muzyka
Robert Onyrscuk

Advertising Sales
George Campbell
Chief
Amy Manning
Director
Jennifer Feidt
Coordinator

©yearBOOKS,Inc.
1 TFH Plaza
Neptune, N.J.07753
Completely manufactured
in Neptune, N.J.

INTRODUCTION by W. P. Mara, Editor

The Green Iguana, *Iguana iguana*, is, without question, one of the most popular herptiles in the world. Kids seem to love them because they look a lot like dinosaurs. Considering the seemingly unlimited popularity of Michael Crichton's riveting novel *Jurassic Park* and its equally absorbing sequel *The Lost World*, it seems anything that has to do with dinosaurs can be a hit these days.

But is it really that simple? Take a look at some other Green Iguana characteristics—newborns are easy to handle and really quite cute, most captives will eat without putting up a fuss (and thrive on a diet of fruits and vegetables, which virtually any keeper can supply without going to any real trouble), and, perhaps most appealing of all, most Green Iguanas, after a period of attentive taming and training, become more of a friend than a pet. You can set one on your desk as you do your homework or carry it on your shoulder. Like a dog or a cat, a Green Iguana has the ability to become more than just a novelty.

In the following pages, experienced keeper and author R. M. Smith will supply you with just about all the information you'll ever need to know about Green Iguanas. You'll learn about their housing, their feeding, their breeding, and even details about their body. When you're done, you'll be something of a Green Iguana expert in your own right, and in the long run, both you and your pets will benefit from that.

What are Quarterlies?

Because keeping reptiles as pets is growing at a rapid pace, information on their selection, care, and breeding is vitally needed in the marketplace. Books, the usual way information of this sort is transmitted, can be too slow. Sometimes by the time a book is written and published, the material contained therein is a year or two old...and no new material has been added during that time. Only a book in a magazine form can bring breaking stories and current information. A magazine is streamlined in production, so we have adopted certain magazine publishing techniques in the creation of this Quarterly. Magazines also can be much cheaper than books because they are supported by advertising. To combine these assets into a great publication, we issued this Quarterly in both magazine and book format at different prices.

CONTENTS

6 · SELECTING YOUR IGUANA

11 · FEATURES OF THE IGUANA BODY

16 · HOUSING YOUR IGUANA

36 · FEEDING

47 · REPRODUCTION

52 · HANDLING AND TAMING YOUR IGUANA

55 · HEALTH PROBLEMS

IGUANAS IN YOUR HOME

by R. M. Smith

DEDICATION

For my mother and father

SELECTING YOUR IGUANA

The first order of business in selecting an iguana is to avoid being buffaloed by exotic names for what is essentially the same animal. Unless you are truly looking at an entirely different species such as a desert iguana (genus *Dipsosaurus*) or a rhinoceros iguana (genus *Cyclura*), a Green Iguana is a Green Iguana and is known in Latin as *Iguana iguana*. They can come from Mexico, Central America, or South America, and the physical variations often exhibited from specimen to specimen often can be attributed to where each specimen originally came from. With the current increase in captive breeding, the possibility exists that breeders will develop some genuinely unique color variations, but for now, in some instances, the jazzy colors that can cost you two to three times as much are, in fact, juvenile colorations that will diminish and usually disappear completely as the animal grows up.

When selecting a juvenile iguana, common sense would seem to tell you to look for a calm, tractable little guy—one who will tolerate being picked up or held without making a fuss. Unfortunately, in this instance, common sense will lead you astray. Most young reptiles, including iguanas, are born knowing that they are the lunchmeat of the universe

and that their survival depends on running, jumping, climbing, or fighting whenever they are approached by another creature. In short, a normal young iguana that is in good health will do anything to avoid you when you approach him. Where juveniles are concerned, the only calm iguana is one who is debilitated by injury, illness,

starvation, or stress due to shipping or poor cage conditions (or, in rare cases, it already has been hand-tamed by someone with lots of patience and free time). Thus, do not judge a juvenile Green Iguana purely on the way it behaves. Look instead for bright eyes, a plump body, a clean vent, and evidence in the display cage that proper food

Be careful of common (English) names when purchasing a Green Iguana. There is only one true Green Iguana, Latin name *Iguana iguana*, while other members of the iguana family (Iguanidae) have names like the Marine Iguana, the Rhinoceros Iguana, and the Desert Iguana. Photo by Isabelle Francais.

When purchasing an adult Green Iguana, try to find one that has been raised in captivity and also has been hand-tamed. Large Green Iguanas that have not had a lot of interaction with humans will be irascible and, consequently, dangerous. Photo by Isabelle Francais.

Know your 'technical terminology' when buying a Green Iguana. 'Captive-*hatched*' doesn't necessarily mean 'captive-*bred*.' It could simply mean the animal was born in captivity from eggs laid by a wild-caught female. Also 'farm-raised' does not necessarily mean the Green Iguana born and raised in captivity (on a farm). It could mean the animal was caught in the wild when young and then maintained for a year or so in an outdoor facility. Photo by Isabelle Francais.

and water has been provided.

If you're selecting an older or larger iguana, your best bet is to buy one from another individual or from a pet shop that you are sure offers specimens captive-bred and raised and have been tamed. An older iguana that has been wild-caught can be a vicious and sometimes dangerous animal to deal with, and often such animals will not be in the best of health at the time of acquisition.

When making your selection, it's always a good idea to check

for broken toes, crest spikes, and missing portions of the tail. However, don't dismiss an individual because of superficial blemishes. Even if an iguana has a few dings on him, he will still make a great buddy and be just as interesting to observe and share your home with as a more perfect specimen.

If, however, the animal seems to be more than just superficially distressed, the general wisdom is not to adopt him. This can be easier said than done—if you really care

for reptiles, sooner or later you're going to take home a creature that you know won't survive if he's left where he is. If you're selecting an iguana that you just can't help rescuing, know that you'll be taking a gamble. However, in many cases, rehabilitating an animal comes to practicing common sense husbandry and one or two veterinary checkups. Plus, you'll have the added satisfaction of having saved a little green life.

An important thing to remember is that your iguana's "stuff" will *always* cost more than the iguana himself. Properly caring for an iguana means a cage of adequate size (large!), food, water, and soaking bowls, appropriate heating and lighting equipment, thermometers, good fresh food—and the willingness to log some time each week preparing the food. These things aren't luxuries— they are vital, and your iguana will not thrive without them.

In the past, iguanas used to be an investment-grade purchase, and the people who bought them had already spent so much money that they didn't balk at spending for the rest of the necessities. These days, however, the animals themselves are so cheap that they can be easily purchased by just about anybody. In addition, iguanas are routinely being sold as a good "beginner's" lizard, which they are most definitely *not*—their dietary requirements are far more difficult to accommodate than those of the average carnivore. In other words, if you're not prepared to do what you need to do and spend what you need to spend, then don't get the iguana.

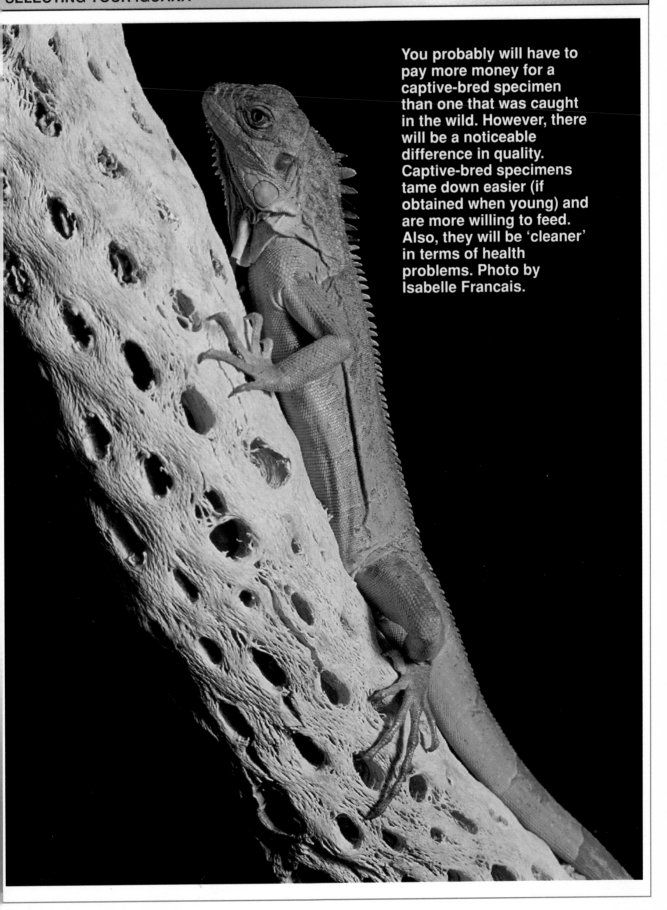

You probably will have to pay more money for a captive-bred specimen than one that was caught in the wild. However, there will be a noticeable difference in quality. Captive-bred specimens tame down easier (if obtained when young) and are more willing to feed. Also, they will be 'cleaner' in terms of health problems. Photo by Isabelle Francais.

Any recently purchased Green Iguanas should be brought to a vet for a thorough initial checkup. By doing this, you assure that any developing health problems are caught in their earliest stages. Photo by Isabelle Francais.

FEATURES OF THE IGUANA BODY

Shedding

Iguanas shed their skin in patches and are essentially shedding all the time. They rarely encounter any difficulties, but there are a few things you will need to check on from time to time. When an iguana is shedding the skin around his eyes, it can be very irritating to him, and you may see him attempting to dislodge the skin by clawing at it or by rubbing his face against things in his cage. This peeling skin causes no problems, but you can make him more comfortable by gently peeling it off yourself.

One place where more serious difficulties can occur is in shedding the coverings of his spines or, more to the point, failing to shed them. The spines are the last thing to be shed as molting progresses, so don't jump the gun and rush to remove them before they are ready. However, if enough time passes and they fail to come off naturally, you will have to help. In many cases, a gentle tug will remove them, but if they do not come off freely, apply a little antibiotic ointment, leave it on overnight, then try again the following day. Bathing the iguana and lightly massaging the old covers may also be helpful. Old spine covers left in place for a long time can ultimately deform the spines—once the spines have become deformed, subsequent shedding will become even more difficult and the

Unlike snakes, many lizards, Green Iguanas included, shed in patches rather than in one whole piece. If you should spot any unshed pieces still stuck to your Green Iguana's body (which happens rather frequently on the spines), you should make every effort to remove them so the animal's skin does not become infected. Photo by K. H. Switak.

problem will be self-perpetuating. If this situation has already developed, you often will be able to see a number of old retained spine covers stacked up in layers around the spine. This kind of buildup can be impossible to deal with without pulling much too hard on the spine—you will have to remove the covers by slipping one blade of a pair of small cuticle scissors between the spine and the old cover(s) and snipping them. Once they have been cut, they should slide off easily.

Watch also for retained skin around the toes. Normal movements by your iguana will tend to knock the old skin off without any problems, but occasionally a

Many people do not realize that Green Iguanas have a third eye. It is not plainly visible from the outside because it is buried deep beneath the skin. It is generally believed this third eye can do little more than distinguish light from dark, although perhaps it once played a greater role many thousands of years ago. Photo by Isabelle Francais.

Zealand) and a few lizards, iguanas included. This median eye has some primitive structures that correspond to those of the main eyeballs, but they are buried so deeply beneath the skin that the median eye can do little more than distinguish light and darkness. The median eye is an extension of specialized brain tissue known as the parietal organ, and a perforation in the cranial bone allows this nerve tissue to extend from the brain to a light-sensitive spot on top of the head. This parietal organ exists in close association with another organ known as the pineal organ, which has evolved into a glandular structure in higher vertebrates. Evidence in reptiles suggests that the modest ability of the median eye in sensing light and darkness plays a role in maturation of sexual organs and endocrine glands, particularly the thyroid, and in the regulation of both seasonal rhythms and daily basking behavior.

Salt Glands

Salt glands are specialized structures found in some lizards, most notably the Marine Iguana, *Amblyrhynchus cristatus*, and our friend the Green Iguana. These glands allow the lizard to minimize water loss and make the most of what's available in his environment. If the metal salts such as those of potassium and sodium that these animals ingest were to be processed through normal digestive means, the osmotic pressure exerted by the salts

few layers of old skin can be retained which will lead to constriction of the toes, and potentially to dry gangrene and loss of the affected toes. These layers of skin are very easy to remove by hand—just check your iguana periodically so they don't build up. Shedding will slow with age but never ceases altogether, and retention of old skin can occur more frequently with older animals, so you'll want to do skin-checks throughout the life of your iguana.

The Parietal Eye

In addition to the two standard eyes at the front of the head, iguanas have a third eye known as the median, or parietal, eye. This eye was a standard feature of ancestral vertebrates—due to its location directly on top of the head, it no doubt provided early swamp-dwellers with a much-needed view of threats from above. This third-eye configuration ultimately passed out of favor, and is now found only in the tuatara (a lizard-like reptile from New

The dewlap is an obvious feature of Green Iguanas, particularly on adult males. The dewlap can be extended with the aid of something called the hyoid bone and is displayed during territorial battles and courtship rituals. Photo by Isabelle Francais.

would quickly lead to dehydration and death. To prevent this, the salt gland accumulates fluid containing the salts to be excreted within a pocket just inside the opening of the nasal passages. The water component of this fluid evaporates as inhaled air passes over it, which serves to both concentrate the salts and humidify the air that the lizard breathes. When enough water has evaporated, the lizard rids itself of the remaining material by sneezing.

The salt gland system is very efficient. The salts are excreted at very high concentration, and almost all the water used as a carrier medium is recovered, which is a great help to life in an arid environment. In captivity, however, the sneezing associated with salt removal can be a source of confusion. If you're not expecting it, hearing the first sneeze from your iguana can make you think he's developed respiratory problems and, conversely, becoming used to hearing him sneeze can lead you to ignore signs of real respiratory distress. This is simply another area where there is no substitute for good daily observations of your animal. A salt-gland sneeze will yield a fine spray from the nostrils, and leave little salty dots on the sides of the cage, and there should be no sounds of labored breathing or other signs of discharge from the animal's nose or mouth. If you have any doubts about what's going on with your iguana, listen to his chest—if he is in respiratory distress, you will hear wheezing and clicking sounds from his chest when he breathes.

One of the most conspicuous features of a Green Iguana's body is the large subtympanic (below the eardrum) scale. This is a characteristic of the species and does not exist on specimens of the other *Iguana* species, *Iguana delicatissima* (the Antillean Iguana). Photo by John Dommers.

The claws of a Green Iguana can be very sharp and therefore should be clipped every now and then by the keeper. Unclipped claws can cause painful rips in the human skin and, when dirty, will consequently cause nasty infections. Photo above by Isabelle Francais. Photo below by W. P. Mara.

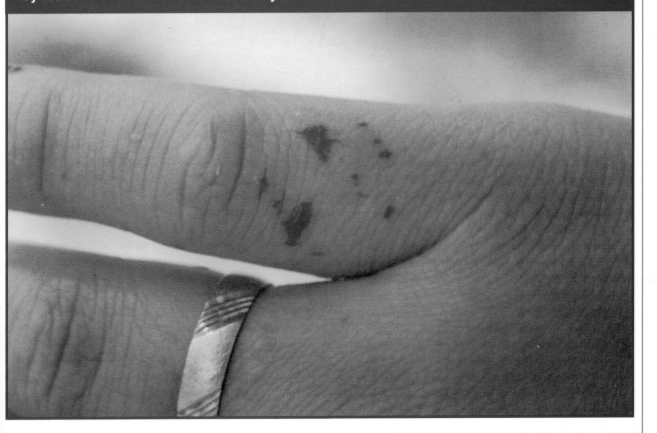

HOUSING YOUR IGUANA

Your new iguana will need a home, of course, and it's tempting to buy an aquarium for him and slap a screen top on it. There are drawbacks to this setup, however—little iguanas will hang from the screen top, either tearing it and escaping or falling from it. Sometimes they catch their tiny claws in it, breaking nails or toes (or both).

Another drawback to the use of an aquarium is that no matter *what* size you get, it will be outgrown within a very short amount of time, and it is axiomatic that when you're guessing what size you need, you will always guess too small. If you already have an aquarium at home, you can probably get by with it for at least a while, but if you need to buy something, buy a good-sized cage *first*. It might seem like overkill when your iguana is small, but it will save you money in the long run to buy a cage he can live in forever, rather than buying a bunch of cages along the way as he outgrows each one.

Furnishing The Cage

Your iguana's cage will need to have some areas for privacy, particularly if you are housing more than one iguana in the same cage. Iguanas generally are not mean lizards, but they have rigid ideas about social hierarchies and will contend with each other to establish dominance. These contests for dominance don't neces-

sarily take the form of actual physical fights (although they can) but they can be a source of intense stress if there are no areas where they can get away from each other for a while. Other than small juveniles, housing more than one iguana in the same cage can be risky business, so keep a close eye on iguanas that are caged together—if you have dominance contests to the point that one or more of them isn't being allowed to feed or use the basking area, you will have to separate them. A lone iguana may decide to get into dominance contests with you since there aren't any other iguanas for him to

"bully." Be firm if his dominance displays threaten your training program (or just head-bob right back at him and enjoy his show).

You will need to provide some pathways through the cage by covering slippery surfaces with burlap, canvas, strong netting, or indoor/outdoor carpeting. The urge to climb is so strong in iguanas that even without a secure foothold, they will keep trying to climb on any slippery stuff no matter how many times they fall off. Put up shelves or ledges at various heights to provide multiple areas for sitting and sleeping. Give your iguana some sturdy branches to

A Green Iguana's cage need not be elaborately furnished. As long as you provide the essentials—a waterbowl, some climbing branches, a substrate, and a rock or two—your animals should do well. Photo by Isabelle Francais.

Some keepers like to give their Green Iguanas free range of their household. As long as the animal has been trained not to destroy furnishings and knows where (and where not) to defecate, this arrangement normally works out fine. Photo by Isabelle Francais.

Keeping an eye on the ambient temperature of your Green Iguana's enclosure is an important facet of good husbandry. If the animal is allowed to become too warm or too cold, it could become ill. Fortunately, high-range thermometers designed specifically for herp-keeping are now available. Photo courtesy of Ocean Nutrition.

become worn or soiled, just slice away the sealant with a razor blade and install new branches.

Providing things for your iguana to do will not only give you a great deal of entertainment in watching him, it is also necessary for his mental well-being to have some things to play on. If you do macrame or know someone who does, you can construct an interesting jungle gym out of sturdy rope. Of course, if you're not handy crafts-wise, you can still make a completely acceptable installation just by knotting some rope to-gether—it might not look as fancy, but your iguana won't mind a bit. The temptation is always strong to use live plants for decor in a lizard's cage, but don't give in to it. They look nice and will help

climb and sit on, particularly within the basking area. Your pet shop will probably have a good selection of branches that you can choose from. Avoid stuff that's been lying on the ground—it will most likely be rotten inside and/or full of bugs. Likewise, avoid small, thin, or brittle branches that may break when the iguana attempts to use them. Most important, do not use branches from resinous or aromatic trees such as pine, cedar, redwood, fir, or euca-lyptus—the oils can cause extremely serious respiratory problems in reptiles. To prevent injuries and make the installation safe for climbing, secure the branches to the floor or sides of the cage by gluing them down with silicone aquarium sealant. When the branches

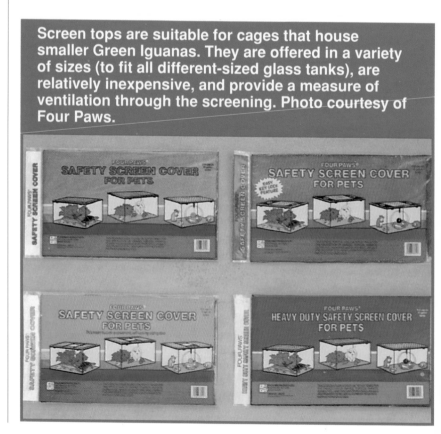

Screen tops are suitable for cages that house smaller Green Iguanas. They are offered in a variety of sizes (to fit all different-sized glass tanks), are relatively inexpensive, and provide a measure of ventilation through the screening. Photo courtesy of Four Paws.

Very large Green Iguanas can be kept in an outdoor pen, but you probably will have to do a bit of carpentry work to provide such an enclosure. On the other hand, a correctly built and furnished outdoor enclosure will be much appreciated by your pets during the warmer months. Photo by Isabelle Francais.

to stabilize humidity to some extent, but they instantly will be munched on and trampled. In addition, few plants are sturdy enough to permit safe climbing, and many seemingly innocuous houseplants are quite poisonous—not a good thing to have around a plant-eater like a Green Iguana.

Heat

Like any tropical reptile, iguanas need substantial heat. First of all, heat needs to be supplied in a gradient so that one end of the cage provides maximum heat while the other end provides the minimum allowable temperature. In addition, a smaller high-temperature area should be provided for basking. During the day, the cool end of the cage should be in the mid-70s, the warm end should be in the mid-80s, and the basking area should be in the high 80s to mid-90s. At night, the cool side should be in the low 70s, and the warm side should be in the low 80s. In the case of juveniles, temperatures at the cool end of the cage or at night should not be allowed to drop below 75°F.

Achieving and maintaining this type of temperature gradient requires careful monitoring, so don't use guesswork—we warm-blooded creatures nearly always tend to estimate things as warmer than they really are. Do it right and use thermometers to check the temperatures at both ends of the cage, and be sure to use the type of thermometer designed for high-temperature use specifically with reptiles— aquarium thermometers designed for tropical fish setups simply don't go high enough to be useful with reptiles. Be sure to place your thermometers at the level occupied by the iguana—putting them anywhere else will give you a deceptive picture of your iguana's cage conditions. Also, place hideboxes in both ends of the cage so your iguana doesn't have to forgo the correct temperature in order to spend time in his box.

Heat can be provided in several ways, and you will probably end up using all of them in order to provide an optimal setup. Iguanas expect to get most of their

In nature, Green Iguanas spend some of their time in water, Thus, you should provide them with a fairly large water body in captivity. A large plastic tub like the one shown will be adequate. Photo by Isabelle Francais.

heat from above, just as they would from the sun in their natural environment.

One popular and highly efficient way to provide this is by using something called a ceramic heater. Ceramic heaters are a very effective and economical means of providing heat, but they do require a few special precautions. Because of the large degree of heat generated, a ceramic heater cannot be used inside a standard reflector hood. Instead, they require a special hood with a heavy-duty ceramic socket that can withstand the heat. You can scale back the heat at night by placing a rheostat in the heater's power line, but make sure you buy one rated for sufficient amperage. Ceramic heaters draw a lot more current than a comparably-sized light bulb, and using devices that are not rated for sufficient amperage easily can start a fire.

Since Green Iguanas are climbers, they *must* have branches in their enclosures. Without them, they will become highly stressed and in turn will be disappointing captives. Photo by Isabelle Francais.

Heated rocks and caves are suitable for the interior of your tank, and undertank heaters will warm the entire habitat. Photo courtesy of Four Paws.

Everybody has made due at one time or another with plain old light bulbs to provide heat. A light bulb will always do in a pinch, but using a ceramic heater that emits nothing *but* heat is much more economical. In addition, light bulbs have their own hazards. Never, for example, use spotlights. Their "spot" characteristics come from having a focusing point for the light, and this point will focus a searing beam on one small area of your iguana's skin, quickly

Choosing the correct enclosure size for your Green Iguanas is a critically important consideration. This 10-gallon tank, for example, probably is too small to suit the fancy of the two young Green Iguanas that are in it. Also keep in mind that Green Iguanas will grow very fast and therefore will need progressively larger enclosures in a relatively short time. Thus, it probably is best to purchase a fairly large enclosure from the start and let your animal(s) 'grow into it.' Photo by Isabelle Francais.

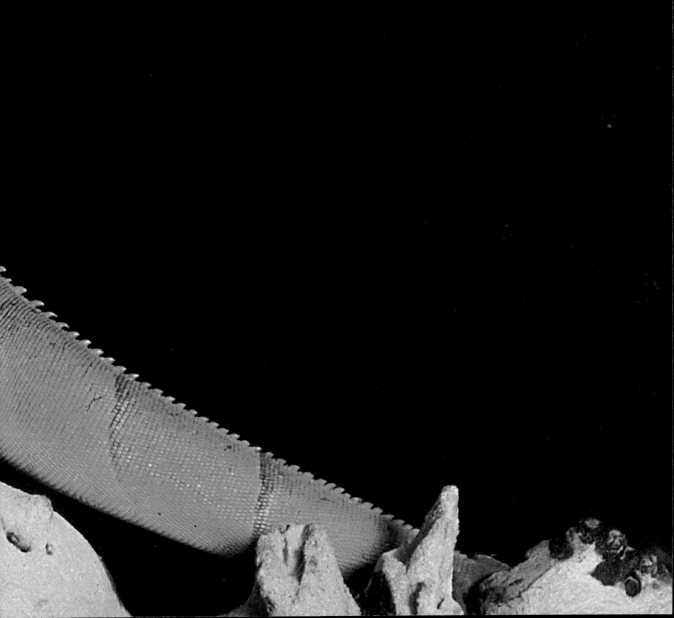

Being from tropical regions, Green Iguanas need a great deal of heat in order to thrive. Fortunately, this can be provided many ways. Ideally, you should arrange for your Green Iguana's enclosure to have multiple temperature zones so the animal can freely choose where it wants to be. Photo by Isabelle Francais.

causing a harmful thermal burn. Other types of light bulbs can also have focusing points without being designated as spotlights, so use caution—iguanas take their own temperature by making a whole-body assessment and can severely burn themselves locally while trying to according to the manufacturer's instructions.

While most of the overhead and basking-spot heat will come from your ceramic heaters, you will still need something to provide a bit of heat from underneath to take the chill off the cage floor. You can accomplish this with one have caused many serious thermal burns in reptiles due to too much heat applied directly against the reptile's skin. In a cage that is too cold, the drive to heat up their insides is so strong that they will seemingly ignore serious thermal burns until a great deal of damage

Since Green Iguanas are inveterate 'baskers,' it is strongly advised that you provide them with a basking site, such as the branch of a tree or a large stone. This area can be warmed with the aid of a spot lamp or similar. Photo by Isabelle Francais.

warm up systemically. You've also no doubt seen (or rigged up yourself) one of those electrical setups consisting of several multi-outlet power strips with extensions cords festooned everywhere—avoid this sort of arrangement with your ceramic heaters. You can jerry-rig light bulbs all day long and usually get away with it, but you should install your heaters only of the many under-tank heating pads available specifically for reptile use, or by using flexible heat tape which can be cut and configured to suit the size of your cage. Either type of under-floor heating should not cover the entire floor but instead leave one section of the tank cooler than the other.

And now, a word about heated rocks. Heated rocks has been done. Many wild lizards get their heat from above (i.e., from the sun), not below. If you have a heated rock and your iguana appears to just love it, you can be utterly sure that his whole cage temperature is too low—the sight of a poor cold iguana clinging desperately to a heated rock means that you need to do some serious revamping of your

Iguanas can be kept together in large groups, but all the specimens should be of similar size. Small specimens kept with large specimens often die from attacks by the latter who are competing for territory. Photo by Isabelle Francais.

heating methods to get the cage temperature up to where it needs to be. If you really want to provide some type of belly heat, put a small pile of smooth river rocks in the cage underneath the path of one of the ceramic heaters—the heat radiated by the heater will warm the rocks naturally, then your iguana can sit on them if he so chooses.

Light

You must provide light of two different types for your iguana—regular light so he knows that it's daytime, and full-spectrum light for proper function of his metabolic processes.

Normal periods of light and dark must be established for your iguana's physical and mental well-being. Without the visual cues provided by a normal day's light and darkness, everything from appetite to hormonal cycles will be disrupted. A normal iguana day should consist of twelve to fourteen hours of light, so you will need to either control the lights yourself or put them on timers. When it's bedtime for your iguana, it should be dark. Even if he sleeps in a hidebox, visible light will place unnecessary stress on him, screwing up his circadian, or daily,

rhythms. Anyone who has napped in a brightly-lit room knows that the quality of their sleep is not the same as if they were in bed in a darkened room, and it's the same for your iguana—don't ask him to get his rest in a brightly-lit room, even if you enjoy being able to view him late at night.

Providing your Green Iguana with the correct photoperiod (day/night cycle) is very important. Photoperiod is often a factor in determining a herptile's behaviorisms, as is the efficient provision of full-spectrum lighting. Bulbs designed specifically for the keeping of reptiles and amphibians now are available at many pet shops. Photo courtesy of Energy Savers.

The other type of light that's critical to your iguana's health is full-spectrum. Full-spectrum plays an important role in both the metabolism of dietary calcium and in ensuring general well-being. One way to provide full-spectrum light is through the use of special bulbs designed particularly for this purpose. Such bulbs can be found in many pet shops. There are also a few incandescent bulbs that are sold with the implication that they provide full-spectrum light, but a tungsten fila-

ment simply is not able to produce the wavelengths of full-spectrum light. "Full-spectrum" simply means the visible wavelengths of normal daylight, i.e., full-spectrum light is essentially the same as that given off by the sun.

Your best bet will be to buy a fluorescent bulb that specifically states that it provides full-spectrum light for use in reptile care and to use it as an adjunct to real sunlight. You can provide genuine sunlight by placing your iguana's cage near a window, or by having an outdoor basking cage for him to use as climate allows. (Be careful, however, that the enclosure doesn't overheat, causing the inmates to roast.) Use your full-spectrum bulb when the weather doesn't permit basking in natural sunlight, and supplement the diet with appropriate vitamins and calcium year-round. Also be aware that natural sunlight loses most of its beneficial qualities when shining through glass. The glass acts as a filter, rendering the light basically useless to a Green Iguana.

Your fluorescent bulb will provide a useful supplement

In the wild, Green Iguanas don't bask in sunlight only for the warmth. Sunlight also plays a role in many physiological processes, including the efficient metabolism of calcium. Thus, unless your Green Iguana is kept outdoors all year long, the provision of full-spectrum light is a must. Photo by Isabelle Francais.

when natural sunlight is not available, but it has certain limitations—as the bulb ages, its output slowly degrades, and the shortwave full-spectrum portion is the first to go even though the visible output looks the same. Since you'll have no way to visually judge when full-spectrum output has begun to fall off, a good

called the inverse-square law, a formula which governs various types of radiation. To understand its implications, imagine doubling the distance between your bulb and its target. Common sense would seem to indicate that twice the distance would produce half the incident light, but it doesn't—twice the distance

from the full-spectrum bulb most of the time.

Owners of iguanas (and other large lizards) are frequently cautioned that exposure to full-spectrum light, in particular to natural sunlight, can result in increased aggressiveness. Sunlight can, in fact, cause temporary behavioral changes and heightened

Green Iguanas kept in glass tanks are in particular need of bulb-generated full-spectrum light because the glass in the their enclosures will filter out most of the beneficial qualities of natural sunlight. You cannot simply park their tank next to a sunlit window. Photo by Isabelle Francais.

general rule is to use the bulb for half its rated lifespan—when that period has elapsed, use the remaining life of the bulb for your house plants, and buy your iguana a new bulb.

When depending on a bulb for the provision of full-spectrum light, the placement of the bulb can make a huge difference in the benefits available from it. Light falls off over distance in accordance with something

produces 1/4 the light, or $1/2^2$. Likewise, tripling the distance results in 1/9th the incident light, or $1/3^2$, and so on. Thus you can see that relatively small changes in the distance from light bulb to iguana can result in pretty drastic changes in the amount of light he actually receives, something to bear in mind when setting up your iguana cage. Ideally, you'll want your iguana to be about four to six feet away

activity, but these changes should be welcomed—you will be seeing the natural animal. To deny your iguana sunlight because you don't want to deal with his increased level of activity is akin to keeping your dog drugged all the time because his docility makes him so much easier to handle. Give your iguana the sunlight he needs and enjoy him for his natural behavior.

If you've gone to the trouble of setting up an outdoor enclosure for your Green Iguana, bring the animal there in a cloth sack rather than carry it in your arms. If it gets away from you, you may have a very hard time getting it back! Photo by Isabelle Francais.

Substrate

Providing a proper substrate for reptile cages has always been something of a challenge as there are many things that appear to be quite useful but are, in fact, dangerous or lethal to your iguana. Iguanas touch everything with their tongues in it is absorbent and harmless to ingest. However, it will rapidly grow molds and fungus wherever it is in contact with moisture, either from feces or spilled water. Because of this propensity for growing instant mold, any pellets with feces or water on them must be kind of commercial cage liner which can be cleaned quite easily and even machine-washed. Alternatively, you can even use paper towels or cloth towels—these might not be as aesthetically pleasing, but they will keep your iguana clean, dry, and healthy, which is what counts.

If you plan to keep your Green Iguana in a naturalistic setup, be aware that Green Iguanas like to taste things with their tongues. Bits of 'loose' substrate like gravel or corn cob may end up in the animal's stomach. Photo by Isabelle Francais.

order to taste and smell their environment, and anything that *can* be picked up and ingested *will* be. Ingestion of any of these materials will lead to stomach upsets, gastrointestinal obstructions and, most likely, death. Keep this in mind when choosing a bedding for the animal's cage.

Some people have used things like rabbit chow since removed immediately. If you use alfalfa pellets, you'll want to clean them up often anyway—the pellets smell nice and green and clean when you first open the bag, and they stink to high heaven once they've been in use for even a short amount of time. In general, the best solution is to use flat woven or pressed indoor/outdoor carpeting or an appropriate

Cleaning The Cage

Cleaning the cage is mostly a matter of common sense—if it looks or smells dirty, it is. For routine clean-ups, all you really need to do is swap the dirty bedding for clean bedding and wipe off any soil or droppings from the cage itself with a damp cloth. You will need to give the cage a more thorough cleaning

Whether you feel it necessary or not, a Green Iguana's tank should be given a thorough cleaning every other week. Cleanliness is one of the most important aspects of efficient husbandry. A heavily diluted bleach/soap/water mixture will do the trick, and remember to rinse the tank *very thoroughly* afterwards. Photo by Isabelle Francais.

periodically, at which time you can use a nontoxic cage cleaner. Most household cleaning products, and any phenol-containing cleaning products, are deadly to reptiles. If you really feel the need for gung-ho cleaning, use a dilute solution of chlorine bleach (1 cup of bleach to 1 gallon of water) and rinse *thoroughly*, i.e.,

until all the bleach residue is gone.

The best way to clean cages is with a set of implements specifically set aside for this purpose. A bucket, a sponge, and some paper towels should cover pretty much all of your equipment needs, but they should be items that have never been in contact with any household cleaning compounds, and they should not be used for anything other than cage care. A good way to keep your iguana-cleaning gear separate is to color-code it—get your sponges, scrubbers, buckets, rubber gloves, etc., all in the same color, and you'll know at a glance that this stash of implements is reptile stuff and not people stuff. Also, if you have a quarantine cage set up for new or sick animals, keep a separate set of cleaning materials (in a different color) for use with that cage as well—mixing up the cleaning tools will spread whatever germs you're trying to quarantine to the other cages and defeat the whole purpose of cleaning in the first place. Gloves are not particularly necessary for cage-cleaning, but if you choose to wear them, the latex surgical-type will leave you much nimbler than rubber dish-gloves do.

The 'Electrical Engineering' Aspect of Housing

When you set up your Green Iguana's cage, all timers, wiring, and fixtures should be on the outside—if they are within reach of the inmates, they will be climbed on just like anything else, and the potential for burns, falls, and electrocutions is

great. Since even the most well-constructed cage is a mix of electrical devices and nearby water, you should use ground-fault interrupters on the circuits that power the equipment. Ground-fault interrupters are those little devices that are now required in all bathroom circuits where the potential for electrocution is high due to the proximity of water—they will clamp the voltage in a circuit within a fraction of a second, and when used on your cage-equipment circuit they will protect both you and your iguana.

Speaking of protection, you should have a disaster plan

If you are looking for a substrate that is lightweight and can be used repeatedly, a terrarium liner will do nicely. Many pet shops now carry these in different sizes so to fit all different enclosures. Photo courtesy of Four Paws.

FEEDING

What Not To Feed

Providing a good diet for your iguana is the most important thing you can do for him—as is the case with human vegetarians, greater care must go into providing proper nutrition than is necessary for carnivores. Part of this preparation includes understanding how your iguana sees his food. As befits a browsing leaf-eater, his color vision is strongest at the red-orange-yellow-green end of the spectrum, which is why he will be tempted by orange squash and dark leafy greens more readily than by boiled white beans.

As a general guideline, adult iguanas should be fed approximately one cup of finely chopped vegetables per day. For smaller iguanas, adjust the amount downward—unlike some of the greedier carnivorous reptiles, iguanas almost never overeat. The diet-related problems which iguanas can experience—and they are numerous—are caused by feeding the wrong foods, not by overeating.

Planning an iguana diet is not simply a matter of picking up whatever looks interesting in the produce section. A number of items that look like perfectly reasonable choices do, in fact, vary from the nutritionally useless to the outright lethal. The things you must avoid, to one extent or another, are kale, broccoli, bok choy, cabbage, brussels sprouts, and cauliflower. These vegetables depress thyroid function and appear to inhibit calcium uptake, which will cause extremely serious illness in your iguana. On their way to causing extreme skeletal deformation and death in your iguana, they will also produce severe muscle and joint pain as the deficiencies they create progress.

Tomatoes, watermelon, other watery vegetables are basically non-foods. You can sprinkle a bit of any of them on top of the real food to add visual appeal, but by themselves they have virtually no nutritional content.

Fruits are another item that will add appeal to the main course or make a fine occasional treat, but are not suitable for a steady diet. They, too, are mostly water (with a lot of sugar) and provide little in the way of good nutrition. In addition, the high sugar content can cause an overgrowth of intestinal bacteria which can produce serious gas and bloating problems. Fruits also tend to have unacceptably high levels of phosphorus.

Spinach contains high levels of oxalic acid, which forms spiky crystals within the delicate structures of the kidneys and can cause permanent damage to them. And rhubarb—any part, in any form—is toxic and must be avoided.

Lettuce is the biggest offender in iguana diets—it is, without a doubt, the single worst thing you can feed your iguana. Lettuce has no calories, no vitamins, and no nutrition. A diet of lettuce will also produce an addiction to it, and it will be difficult to wean a lettuce-craving iguana onto a proper diet. A little

Adult Green Iguanas are much more herbivorous than the young and should be fed about one cup of finely chopped vegetables per day. They can be given the occasional fruit as a treat, but most fruits should not be offered as part of the main diet. Photo by Isabelle Francais.

Most Green Iguanas will gladly accept pieces of iceberg lettuce, but, as many keepers already know, iceberg lettuce has virtually no nutritional value. Most lettuces, in fact, should be avoided in the Green Iguana diet, but if your animal has already developed a liking for it, use the romaine variety, which is the most nutritious form. Photo by John Dommers.

female specimen I once saw was stunted to roughly one-fourth her normal size and was left with massive facial and skeletal deformities due to a diet of mainly lettuce with some spinach and cauliflower thrown in—a lethal combination, and the effects were clearly visible. Also, it is not just head or iceberg lettuce that does the damage—lettuce is lettuce, be it iceberg, butter lettuce, head lettuce, red or green leaf, or romaine lettuce (although romaine certainly is the most nutritious of the bunch).

Another extremely damaging dietary item is animal protein. Feeding protein-rich items such as dog chow, cat chow, or monkey chow, crickets, worms, mice, or other animal protein sources will cause extremely rapid growth in iguanas. It seems to be human nature to associate rapid growth with health and hardiness, but the large iguanas built with protein diets will die in roughly half the time they normally would.

In the past, it was commonly thought that juvenile iguanas would consume relatively large amounts of animal protein, mostly in the form of bugs before tapering off to an herbivorous diet as they grew up. While the amount of research done on proper iguana diets is still underwhelming, what has been done seems to indicate that a herbivorous diet is the right thing to feed from youth to old age.

Finally, anecdotal stories are always going around about iguanas who like pizza or quiche or slices of cheese, etc. Unfortunately, there are some keepers who actually brag about the various bizarre items that they have fed to their iguanas. Perhaps they are counting on the old wives' tale that animals know what's good for them—e.g., if their iguana will eat it, it must be okay. In reality, an animal in its natural habitat will know what to eat and what not to eat, but an animal removed from its natural habitat won't have a clue as to what's safe and nutritious. So, avoid cheese (too high in salt and fat,) tofu (too oily,) experiments with house and garden plants (potentially toxic,) and any other oddball

As with any other herptile, a Green Iguana should not be fed only one item but rather a mixture of many. You will have to experiment to find out which nutritious foods your pet prefers, but in the end it will be worth it. Remember—the more varied the diet, the better. Photo by Isabelle Francais.

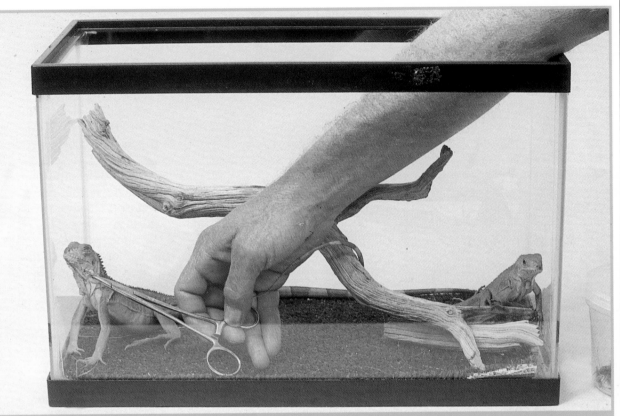

Young Green Iguanas are at least partially carnivorous and therefore can be offered the occasional mealworm or waxworm. Keep in mind, however, that current research suggests the possibility that even the youngest Green Iguanas need very little in the way of animal proteins, so don't overdo it. Offer livefood items only as a treat. Photo by Isabelle Francais.

items. You might have a few less anecdotes to tell, but you'll have an iguana that's alive and healthy.

What To Feed

For folivores (leaf-eaters) such as iguanas, leafy green vegetables are the best approximation of their natural diet at the keeper's disposal. Your basic staple diet should consist of one leafy green vegetable, one orange vegetable, a bit of fruit, and a bit of protein, with calcium and vitamin supplements added about twice a week. For greens, choose snow or snap peas (the kind with the edible pods), green beans, carrot or

beet tops, parsley, and turnip, mustard, or collard greens. Collard greens in particular are an excellent choice as they are very high in calcium. Freshness is important in all food items, but particularly so in leafy greens as they lose their nutrients quite rapidly as they age. The general rule for ascertaining the state of freshness in leafy greens is, if it looks cruddy, it is. Wilting, yellowing of the leaves, and the other visible signs of loss of freshness are readily apparent—if it no longer looks fresh and appetizing, then it's no longer fresh enough to serve to your iguana. Premature demise of your

leafy greens can be avoided to some extent by using the type of vegetable-storage bags that have tiny holes throughout the bag—they actually do help retain freshness and keep the greens looking good.

For orange vegetables, choose carrots or whatever type of squash is seasonally available in your area. Butternut squashes are a particular favorite with iguanas and are available virtually year-round. Sweet potatoes are also good (cooked and mashed) and are much better than yams—yams, while not particularly harmful, are much poorer in nutrients than are sweet potatoes.

Animal protein should be less than 2% of the diet of an adult iguana, but protein from other sources is still necessary. Iguanas in their natural environment get their protein from plant sources such as the leaves of legumes (pea and bean plants), and you can produce a reasonable facsimile by boiling up the peas and/or beans and chopping them up. There are many different kinds of dried beans to choose from at the grocery store—white beans, red beans, black beans, kidney beans, etc.—so boil a variety of them and see which your iguana will take. Be sure to use only beans, peas, or seeds from the grocery store, i.e., those that are intended for human consumption. Peas, seeds, and beans that are intended for seed stock or for farm or garden use are treated with tremendous amounts of pesticides and antifungal compounds and are highly toxic to Green Iguanas. You can also increase the protein content of the basic food bowl by adding textured vegetable protein, available at most health food stores. Soak it in water until it softens and expands, then mix it in with the rest of the iguana chow.

Certain fruits should be another small part of the basic diet. As stated earlier, they aren't so great in the nutrition department, but they add taste and visual appeal and make good occasional treats and rewards. You can choose from strawberries or other berries, cantaloupe, kiwi fruit, grapes, mangos, peaches, pears, plums, apricots, bananas, or whatever else looks good in the produce section. Figs are the best fruits of all because they are so rich in calcium, and dried figs are the richest of all. Soak them until they soften and plump up, then chop them and mix them in with the rest of the food. Leave in the water in which the figs soaked, as well, as it also contains part of the figs' nutrients. Raisins can be fed in the same way, after soaking and plumping.

Additional items which you can use for variety include softened multi-grain bread, okra, mushrooms, mild bell peppers (red), asparagus, moistened alfalfa pellets (rabbit or guinea pig chow), and sprouts of various kinds. Sprouts aren't hugely nutritious on their own, but they make excellent extras for a little variety. You can obtain several different varieties from most health-food stores, or you can sprout your own from beans, alfalfa, lentils, barley, garbanzo beans (chick peas), or unsalted sunflower seeds.

Incidentally, frozen vegetables are another type of food that should be avoided. A little won't hurt, but don't feed frozen stuff as a staple diet. Frozen greens develop thiaminase, an enzyme which slowly destroys the thiamine (B_1) content of the food. This can lead to deficiency disease when frozen foods are fed too frequently. This vitamin loss develops about a week or two after freezing, so if you absolutely have to feed something that's been frozen longer than that, supplement it with reptile vitamins or brewers' yeast to replenish the missing B_1. Frozen vegetables also cost considerably more than their fresh counterparts,

Commercially produced and pre-packaged Green Iguana foods are easy to portion out and store. They are specially formulated to suit the needs of Green Iguanas and can be purchased at many pet shops. Photo courtesy of Ocean Nutrition.

so in general they are not a very good deal monetarily or nutritionally.

Baby food is useful for special situations, although it shouldn't be used as a main component. If you've got some around that you want to use up, you can always toss it into the basic staple mix, but its main use is as a force-feeding food. It is easy to load into a force-feeding syringe due to its consistency, and it's also quite easy to digest. If you're going to use baby food as part of a daily feeding mixture, select the same types of vegetables that you would feed normally, and stay away from the meat items. When force-feeding a sick or wasted iguana, you should also supplement the baby food with some calcium and vitamin supplements.

To prepare your own fresh iguana food, sooner or later you'll want to use some type of food processor. Iguanas have plenty of teeth but do not use them to chew their food, so it will be up to you to chop it into edible form. This means reducing it to small pieces, which enables them to pack more food into their bellies and permits better digestion and utilization of nutrients. You can always get by with scissors or a potato peeler for chopping or shredding, but your life will be infinitely more pleasant if you get some type of food processor—a fancy processor costing several hundred dollars will obviously do a pretty good job, but so will a thirty-dollar "salad shooter."

Mulching up the basic foods in a processor will also make it easier to tinker with your iguana's diet. Many iguanas absolutely hate the taste of

The occasional inclusion of a little calcium powder on your Green Iguana's foodstuffs will do a great deal of good. Young Green Iguanas in particular will need plenty of calcium while they grow through their early years. Photo courtesy of American Reptile.

vitamin and calcium supplements, which are an important part of good nutrition, and you will stand a better chance of slipping them past your iguana if they are mixed throughout his meal. Iguanas are also very good at picking out their favorite items and leaving the rest, but grinding everything up together will make that sort of pickiness virtually impossible.

Fine-chopping of your iguana's dinner will also help you to make dietary changes. For better or worse, iguanas will adapt to almost any type of food, and once they are habituated to a bad diet it can be very hard to wean them off it. This is particularly true of lettuce-addicted iguanas. To wean them away from this harmful food, include some of this 'forbidden' item in the chopped mix, along with the foods that your iguana *should* be eating. Keep in mind that weaning a Green Iguana through a dietary change is not an overnight occurrence, however—keep offering the

new combination until your iguana eats it. He may pitch a fit over it temporarily, but no healthy iguana will turn down good food that's right in front of him.

When you are preparing the food, remove the thick stems from the greens—they can cause gum damage—and always make sure that the food is at room temperature before serving. Feed your iguana as often as he seems hungry—iguanas are natural browsers and feed fairly constantly in nature. Unlike carnivorous reptiles, your iguana can't just pack away a big meal and then sit tight for a few days. This also means that you can't go away for more than a day or so without making provisions for someone else to feed him. Feed your iguana at midday, between 11:00 a.m. and 2:00 p.m. Iguanas aren't ready to feed until they've spent their morning warming themselves up to operating temperature, and they need the remaining afternoon warmth to digest their food. Iguanas are so strongly diurnal that it is disruptive to them to be fed at night, but if for some reason you must feed your iguana late, make sure you keep the heaters and the basking spot fired up so he will have the warmth necessary for digestion.

You may freeze a portion of the feeding mixture for later use (though the same vitamin precautions as with other frozen foods apply), but be sure that all frozen or refrigerated food has reached room temperature all the way through before you feed it. A fast zap in the microwave makes this easy, but check the temperature to make sure it hasn't overheated. There is also nothing wrong whatsoever with freezing, per se—it is the length of time that does the damage. At least when you're making and freezing your own food you'll know how long it's been frozen, as opposed to the stuff in the frozen food case, which could have been there since the last ice age.

A final bit of advice—don't use any of the "vegetable washes" that are now on the market. They haven't been around long enough for us to really know what effects (if any) they might have on reptiles, and too often "100% safe" stuff turns out to be 100% disastrous. Wash your vegetables in tap water, though, since vegetables do grow outside, in the dirt, where they can be susceptible to everything from bugs to bird poop on them.

One last feeding problem you might run into is a lack of appetite. If your iguana is newly acquired and refusing

to eat, it could be for a variety of reasons. Initially, lack of interest in food may indicate nothing more than stress, so begin dealing with the problem not by handling the animal, but by providing an adequate hidebox, by reducing traffic around his cage, and by dimming the lights. In addition, don't spend too much time ogling him—some iguanas are just naturally fussy and won't eat while you're watching or even while you're in the room.

If that doesn't turn out to be the problem, then his cage may be too hot or cold, he may have either an infectious or metabolic disease, his captive conditions may be dirty or inappropriate, or he may have internal parasites. If he is newly acquired, he should be checked for all these things, and an initial visit to a vet is a good idea.

Appetite can sometimes decrease slightly for no apparent reason and then return to normal shortly thereafter. A refusal to feed that persists for two weeks or more becomes cause for concern, as it may lead to malnutrition. Malnutrition appears as little or no growth, a gaunt or wasted appearance, lack of activity, dull skin, and brittle bones which may fracture spontaneously. Malnutrition that is proceeding in this direction will need aggressive intervention—a veterinarian should be consulted as soon as possible and a regimen of supplements and force-feeding worked out. If treatment for this condition is not begun rapidly, the iguana will either die or at the minimum be stunted for the remainder of

his life. Iguanas that have been stunted by poor nutrition, its attendant diseases, and consistent lack of heat will start growing again when the conditions are rectified but will never achieve what would have been their normal size. Even after growth recommences, the animal should be seen by a veterinarian since they will almost certainly have other problems such as bladder stones from their poor diets.

In less serious cases of lack of appetite, try switching the staple diet to something slightly different or garnish it with different brightly-colored bits of food such as chopped mild red bell peppers. The presence of another iguana will often stimulate the appetite of a reluctant eater, so if you have more than one iguana, place their cages so that they can see one another. (If they are two males and appear to be irritating each other after a time, separate them again.) You might also try hand-feeding, but don't overdo it—an iguana can easily get so used to it that he will lose his desire to feed from his bowl, and then you'll have a whole new problem to overcome.

Water

A persistent myth regarding iguanas is that they get all the water they need from their food and do not need an additional source. Perhaps in nature they drink less often due to the availability of water-rich succulent plant foods, but in captivity, daily supplemental water is a must.

Providing water is easy— just give them a filled water bowl each day. It doesn't need

Green Iguanas that refuse to feed can be gently and passively force-fed by having their mouths opened and food placed inside. Afterwards, the mouth should be closed again, and your hands should be slowly removed. Don't actively and aggressively force a Green Iguana to eat, for that will only serve to stress the animal, making it even more unwilling. Photo by Isabelle Francais.

Green Iguanas like to climb around on things in their enclosure, and sometimes they defecate on those things. Thus, something like a waterbowl has to be checked daily. If it is dirty, it should be thoroughly washed and then refilled. A dirty waterbowl is an ideal breeding ground for pathogens. Photo by Isabelle Francais.

o be large, but it does need to
ubstantial enough that it will
ot tip over easily. Heavy-
ottomed ceramic bowls or
on-tip dog or cat bowls will
vork just fine. Iguanas
eldom have any difficulty
nding their water bowl and
earning to drink from it. If
our iguana is a very young
ne, he may need a little more
ime to figure things out, in
vhich case you should mist
he tank with a spray bottle
s well as provide a small
owl. He will be able to drink
rom the droplets of mist
vhile he gets used to the
vater bowl—just make sure to
ise a spray bottle that is
ither brand-new or one
vhich has never had anything
ut water in it. If your iguana,
vhether young or old, still has
lifficulty drinking from his
owl, it may because the bowl
imply is too tall. Get a lower
ne or place a branch or a
ock next to it so the iguana
an gain easy access to it.

Water quality varies
lramatically from region to
egion, and reptiles are so
ensitive to contaminants that
he smart thing to do is give
our iguana bottled water.
\void distilled water—the
listillation process removes
he minerals and trace
lements, which is dandy for
our steam iron but not so
ot for your animals. Instead,
ise the type of water labelled
"drinking" or "artesian" water.
3uying water may seem like a
nuisance, but for a small
xpense each month you can
\void any concerns about the
narmful effects of using tap
vater—cheap insurance for
our pet's well-being. In
ddition, when you mist the
ank with bottled water, you
von't get the unsightly

crusty-looking stuff that tap
water leaves behind when it
dries.

It will be up to you to make
sure that you provide clean
water, and that the water you
provide *remains* clean. With
iguanas, as with many
reptiles, the urge to defecate
in the water can be so strong
that it's not uncommon to
find even a very large iguana
maneuvering himself into
extraordinary positions so he
can take aim at a very small
water bowl. This can make
your life a bit easier, as cage
cleaning then consists of
simply pitching out the
contents of the water bowl.
But it will be up to you to
make sure that a bowl of
contaminated water doesn't
remain in the cage. It is
commonly thought that all
animals will recognize fouled
water and not drink it, but
that isn't true, particularly
with reptiles who can be just
a bit stupid when confronted
with dirty water in their bowl.
Drinking fouled water is
certainly no good for anybody,
but if you have more than one
iguana housed together,
leaving them all with a
contaminated water bowl is a
great way to spread diseases
and parasites. Of course, all
animals will drink dirty water
if they are sufficiently thirsty
and nothing else is available,
so make sure that your
iguana has what he needs.

In addition to drinking
water, iguanas also appreciate
a good soak on a frequent
basis, which can be provided
in several different ways.
Iguanas, like many other large
lizards, like to sit in bathtubs
and soak, but they tend to be
distressed by their inability to
get a foothold on the slick

sides. You can assist them by
using a rubber bathmat on
the bottom, and a towel or
another rubber mat draped
and secured over the edge of
the tub. This will give your
iguana a sense of security
both when he's standing and
when he decides it's time to
climb out. If you do use your
bathtub for iguana-soaking,
be sure that it has no traces
in it of any bathroom cleaners
or scouring products—all are
toxic to reptiles.

Smaller iguanas can soak
quite happily in a hard rubber
dish tub or in any of the many
plastic shoeboxes, sweater
boxes, or storage bins
available these days. If you
use this type of soaking
arrangement inside the
iguana's cage, he will be able
to come and go as he pleases,
using it as needed. You will,
however, need to check on
him from time to time to make
sure that he's not overdoing
it. Iguanas can oversoak
themselves when they are new
or under stress if there are no
other hideboxes or secure
areas provided for them. The
water itself isn't going to do
them any damage, but if the
tub is not in a warm enough
spot, the iguana will cool as
the water cools, and he will
soon be too cold and sluggish
to get out and get warm
again. Thus, you should
always make sure that the
soaking facility is in a nice
toasty spot and never use cool
or cold water to fill it.

Iguanas also like a
relatively humid environment,
which you can easily achieve
by misting your iguana's tank
with a spray bottle—just
make sure that the cage is
allowed to dry out after
misting, and be *sure* to allow

One reason Green Iguanas like the water is because they occasionally like to bathe. In captivity, Green Iguanas do have a tendency to become rather filthy, so it is advised that you also give them warm-water baths every now and then. Photo by Isabelle Francais.

For Green Iguana specimens that are relatively tame and calm, you might want to let them bathe in a slop-sink every now and then. This will give them a chance to get their skin clean, and they'll enjoy the opportunity to swim around as well! (And you should, of course, thoroughly clean the sink afterwards). Photo by Isabelle Francais.

it to dry out before the iguana goes to sleep. If your climate is exceptionally dry, or your tank quite large, you can provide constant humidity by installing a large jar of water in the cage and bubbling air through the water by use of an airstone and a small aquarium pump.

A popular myth is that iguanas (and other reptiles) absorb water through their skins while soaking. This is absolutely untrue. Soaking does, however, keep them clean, make them happy, and help them poop if they've become constipated. Raising the ambient humidity by misting or through the use of the 'bubble-jar' will also soothe and protect the iguana's respiratory system. Nothing, however, will take the place of the drinking water you give him—iguanas, like all animals, can manage a while without food if they must, but they cannot do without daily access to drinking water.

REPRODUCTION

Telling the sexes apart visually is not easy since both sexes look very similar. As adults, male iguanas have substantially larger heads and necks, larger dewlaps, and the femoral pores (the line of 'dots' on the inner thighs) are larger in males than in females (although "larger" and "smaller" can be difficult to judge if you don't have other iguanas with which to compare yours). Colors can also vary, as the males will show color changes during breeding season, and older males will often develop orange coloration on their bodies while females are less prone to color changes as they mature. Males will also have a bulge at the base of their tales where the hemipenes lie, and, as they mature, they become "jowlier" than the females.

Sexual maturity in a well-nourished iguana will occur in two to three years, and the better the diet the sooner it will occur. Breeding behavior consists of plenty of head-bobbing, dewlap-displaying, shows of dominance and territoriality and, not uncommonly, amorous advances towards female keepers. You may also spot your male attempting to rub his femoral pores against objects within his cage. The waxy secretions from these pores are used to mark his territory. He will also attempt to rub them onto any females that happen by. A male putting on his breeding show will also tend to eat quite lightly during this time. The females will answer with some head-bobbing of their own, but they will not undergo the changes in color.

If you are going to allow your iguanas to mate, be sure to provide a lot of room; they'll need it. You also should keep all males apart from each other since their threat

One way to tell males from females is by the size of the femoral pores along the inside of the hind legs. With males, these pores are notably larger. Of course, this is a comparative characteristic, so you'll need two specimens of similar size in order to make the distinction. Photo by Isabelle Francais.

displays can rapidly turn into fights. Injuries can also be severe between males and females, as the male will use his teeth and claws to grasp the female by the back, shoulders, and head to subdue her and mate with her. In fact, many people prefer not to breed their iguanas because the potential for serious injury is always present. Nonetheless, most iguanas survive the preliminaries and proceed to a successful mating.

Young Green Iguanas are very hard to separate sexually because the physical differences are not yet obvious. Often you will have to buy three or four specimens in the hopes that you will end up with at least one pair. Photo by Isabelle Francais.

Once the male has subdued his chosen female, he will insert one of his hemipenes (the paired organs of copulation) into the female's cloaca, or vent, and then mating will be underway. The mating pair may remain in this position for some time and should not be disturbed until they are finished.

A successful mating between two iguanas will, of course, result in eggs. The eggs are fertilized in the upper part of the oviduct and are shelled as they travel further down the oviduct. A gravid (egg-laden) female will start to look girthy throughout her abdomen and will start eating less and less as her internal real estate gets taken up by the developing eggs. She will also become restless and grouchy and should be handled only when absolutely necessary due to the potential for rupture of the eggs.

As egglaying time nears, the gravid female will start searching for a suitable site in which to deposit her eggs. You will need to provide her with a nesting box far enough in advance so that she is able to get familiar with it. Many people use a cat's covered litter box, but you can make a nesting box from scratch as long as it provides plenty of privacy. Some females prefer a nesting box with a tight opening or with a piece of PVC pipe that creates a tunnel entrance.

The nesting box should be filled with a mixture of sphagnum moss and damp sand. The female will want to dig before she lays her eggs, so the nesting medium must allow her to do this. After she has excavated her spot in the

box, she will lay her eggs and then cover them up. The box should be in a warm area to increase its attractiveness to the female. Once the eggs have been laid they should be removed and placed in an incubator. When you remove them, bear in mind that they

Only the healthiest Green Iguana specimens should be used in a captive-breeding program. Those that are not in peak health probably will not be able to withstand the considerable strain of the breeding process. The females, in particular, will experience a great deal of physical stress. Photo by Isabelle Francais.

must remain in the same orientation in which they were laid—rotating the eggs will cause the yolk to smother the embryo, resulting in its death.

Normal egglaying can take quite a while, but if you have reason to suspect that your female has not been able to deposit all her eggs, or if she fails to lay any of them, then you will need to take her to the vet. Egg-binding unfortunately is common in iguanas and is frequently caused by calcium deficiencies which result in improper

shelling of the eggs and in weakness of the muscles used to expel them. Females often will retain their eggs until the eggs pose a health hazard simply for lack of a suitable nesting site, which should have been provided well ahead of time. Regardless of the

cause, egg-retention is a serious medical problem and requires prompt attention.

Egglaying can sometimes be stimulated with a combination of warm baths and injections of oxytocin, but egg-bound females frequently require surgical removal of the eggs, at which time they are also routinely spayed. Spayed females tend to live longer, most likely as a result of being freed from the stresses of reproduction. But even successful surgery is hard on them. Without it, however, the

If you're serious about breeding Green Iguanas, get your specimens when they're in early adulthood (and try to obtain only specimens that have been bred and raised in captivity). That way, you can begin your breeding program at once. Photo by Isabelle Francais.

retained and decomposing eggs will release toxins, cause secondary infections, obstruct the oviduct, and ultimately kill the female. Obviously, the best thing to do is to make every effort to avoid the problem altogether by providing a nutrient-rich diet and an appropriate nesting box.

If you have a female, you will need to keep an eye on her during breeding season even if she has not been mated with a male. Although iguanas don't reliably produce eggs the way a chicken will, an unbred female is perfectly capable of developing a whole bellyful of eggs. She may produce them as a response to the breeding cues and hormonal changes produced by having males visible and within scent distance—or she may do it for no apparent reason at all. In any case, she will need exactly the same

attention as a normally gravid female—the same fortified diet (lots of calcium), the same delicate handling and, most importantly of all, the same nesting box. She can experience the same difficulties with egg-binding as a mated female, and in fact may be more prone to them since, without any suspicion of her pregnancy on your part, you may not know to provide the things she needs in time. If you think your female may be doing some spontaneous egg-making, it's a good idea to take her to the vet for an X-ray, which will give you an idea of how far along she is, what kind of shape the eggs are in, and whether or not you're approaching an emergency situation with retained eggs.

If all goes well, the eggs will begin to develop and, after approximately 90 days at 85°, you will have baby iguanas.

Hatchlings eat the same basic foods that the adults do, but the food obviously must be chopped small. The hatchlings also will most likely not be interested in eating for several days or so after hatching since they will still be absorbing residual yolk from the egg.

It is at this stage that young iguanas will need to acquire the bacteria that will thrive in their gut and assist them in a lifetime of digesting plant material. Under natural circumstances, young iguanas will inoculate themselves with these beneficial bacteria through ingesting a bit of the droppings of the adults in the area. You can use the same method if you are certain that your adults are healthy and parasite-free, but bring a bit of the droppings into the juveniles' cage rather than allow the little ones to mix with the

Green Iguanas that are to be used for future breeding projects should be maintained on a nutrient-rich diet. In particular, gravid specimens that suffer from nutritional deficiencies may fall victim to many unpleasant problems, including egg-binding and the laying of eggs that are infertile. Photo by Isabelle Francais.

adults—adult iguanas will often attack and sometimes even eat the little ones. It is probably not intentional cannibalism—most likely it is simply that the little ones are small and moving and thus look like dinner. If your little iguanas don't get their loading dose of bacteria, or if you've bought a very young juvenile who missed his chance to get it at the iguana farm, digestive problems such as bloating will develop, particularly if there are sugary fruits or complex carbohydrates such as cereal grains in the diet. If you need to mastermind the bacteria situation yourself and the natural method seems unappealing to you, you can obtain appropriate bacteria for inoculation from your veterinarian.

Most iguana owners are thrilled to get even one good hatch in captivity, but if you are successful to the point where you're able to breed further generations, make sure that you do not allow related offspring to breed among themselves. Some animals, most notably rats and mice, can withstand seemingly unlimited matings between siblings and even backcrosses between offspring and parents without any significant genetic deterioration. In iguanas, however, the offspring of a cross between any related animals will show rapid genetic deterioration and loss of vigor. Thus if you continue to breed, make sure that all your matings are outcrosses—that is, matings between completely unrelated individuals.

A Green Iguana's nesting box need not be anything elaborate. This keeper, for example, used a deep, sand-filled bucket. Once the eggs have been laid, however, it is advised that they be removed and placed in an artificial incubator. Photo by Isabelle Francais.

HANDLING AND TAMING YOUR IGUANA

The sooner you make your iguana a part of the family, the sooner he will be healthier and less stressed, and the happier you will be with him. Your iguana will be around as long as or longer than most dogs and will provide you with a great deal of marvelous companionship if he's been trained properly, so start training him as soon as you can. Your iguana will exhibit a lot of responsiveness, but if you merely keep him as a specimen he won't have much fun and neither will you. Enjoying him fully takes interaction, play, and handling—properly tamed, he will become a real part of your family.

When you first approach him he may jump around, whip his tail at you, or snap at you, which can be a pretty intimidating display. A lot of this initial carrying-on is, however, merely a bluff—when you just go ahead and pick him up he will usually stop. It's important to just keep handling him—the whole point of his display is to make you *want* to go away, and you need to make it clear to him early on that it simply isn't going to work. While most attempts to bite are part of the threat display, you will make it harder for him to resist taking a chomp at you if you approach him wearing perfumes or hand lotions. Don't make it harder for him to do what you want—if your scented products attract (or irritate) him into trying to bite you, just wash them off and go right back to working with

him. Taming an iguana gets harder and harder as they get older, so do it when they're young!

When you pick him up, let him straddle your arm—the more you behave like a tree branch, the calmer and more content he'll be. Most iguanas prefer to feel like they've still

handling sessions. However, the gloves can cause you to injure him due to your decreased sensitivity. The solution to the problem is to trim the animal's claws, coat your wounds with hydrogen peroxide, and forget about the gloves. At the most, you should use gauntlet-style

When lifting a Green Iguana (or, for that matter, just about any animal), be sure to give it as much bodily support as possible. If the animal feels as though it might fall, it will writhe and wriggle and probably scratch you in the process. Photo by Isabelle Francais.

got a little control over things, so they will usually sit quietly if they feel supported and safe rather than restricted. Once you and your iguana start getting used to each other, you can enhance his sense of freedom by allowing him to climb around on you.

Since iguana claws can carve painful lacerations in your arms, you may be tempted to use gloves during

gardening gloves and cut off the fingers. Your fingers aren't going to sustain much damage anyway—the scratches will be on your forearm where the iguana hangs.

Arriving at a workable arrangement with your iguana means establishing yourself firmly as the dominant life-form in your household, but it also means using good judgement. Don't try to pick him up when he's eating, don't startle him out of a sound sleep or snatch him out of his hidebox, and don't pick him up if he's already agitated over something. Even though you're the 'head honcho' in the relationship, you need to adjust your demands to suit what he is able to comply with—it won't take long for you to learn how to his moods and respect them.

It's also important to remember that, while you should get an early start on training him, you shouldn't *over*train him. When you attempt to get chummy with an iguana that is too new or too young, he may injure himself in struggling with you or he may just freeze, giving the appearance of submission. What looks like surrender, though, is in fact the freezing of movement that comes from stark terror, and the minute he senses any relaxation on your part he will be off like a shot. When making your approach, covering his head or both his head and body with a towel will often have a calming effect and enable you to handle him more easily—use a smaller, lighter-weight cloth for a small specimen. Take your time when you are picking him up or moving him—limbs and toes are delicate, particularly in young iguanas, and you can injure or break them if you pull your iguana away too roughly when he is clinging to something.

Occasionally even a well-tamed iguana can suddenly appear to revert to untrained behavior, forgetting to use his normal toilet spot, starting to pace or rub his snout, or just generally acting like a delin-

Particularly irascible Green Iguanas should first be grasped in such a way that their limbs are immobilized, as shown here. After that, the tail should be tucked under the handler's arm, and every effort should be made to keep the animal's mouth away from the handler's skin. Photo by Isabelle Francais.

quent. This regression is usually a result of stress from some sort of change in his cage or his life. It can also be a show of his displeasure with you if you have recently taken a vacation or otherwise left him alone. Just resume your old taming methods, and his apparent regression should be short-lived. In any case, however you handle him, make it a pleasant experience for both of you by giving him a treat when you pick him up. Giving him a juicy strawberry or other sweet treat will help him to associate being handled with something enjoyable, which will help you tame him when he's young and make for pleasant interactions throughout his life.

The Free-Range Iguana

Iguanas are both inquisitive and athletic by nature, and permanent confinement to a cage will lead to loss of muscle tone as well as deterioration of their dispositions due to the sheer frustration of it all. In short, you cannot keep an iguana caged all the time any more than you can buy a dog, leave it permanently in a box, and expect it not to go crazy. Permitting some free-range time is suitable only for reasonably tame animals, but learning that they have some freedom and control in their lives will help them to become even calmer and will help to eliminate the restlessness and displays of frustration commonly shown by continuously caged iguanas. Giving them some freedom will also be helpful to you in that they will behave better since they won't be as stressed.

All sorts of interesting products are being designed for the keeper who likes to carry around his or her Green Iguana. Tame specimens can be 'walked' with the aid of a leash. Check with your local pet shop for the availability of such products. Photo courtesy of Ocean Nutrition.

Permitting your iguana some free-range time requires some thoughtfulness—without careful preparation, your house can be a deathtrap for your pet. You should never let your iguana loose in a room with weak or insubstantial window screens. Even fairly small iguanas can rip their way through window-screening in no time flat. And, in any case, small iguanas should not be allowed out at all until they are at least half-grown because there are simply too many dangers around for a small specimen. Iguanas routinely flop out of the trees in their natural environments without doing themselves any harm, but they have little ability to judge distance or height when surrounded by man-made features and virtually no ability to judge the hardness of the floors on which they will land, so it will be up to you to provide for your iguana's safety.

Rather than attempting to rearrange your entire house, the best way to ensure the well-being of your wandering iguana is to fix up (and heat) a safe-room for him. By designating one room in which he can roam to his heart's content, you can make sure it's iguana-proof with a minimum of effort. For a safe-room to be safe, any window screens should be reinforced with welded wire mesh, all nooks, crannies, and holes should be eliminated, and any items which can be pulled over, pulled down, or pulled apart should be removed. Remove all small objects, whether on furniture or floors, as they can easily be ingested during exploration. You should also make certain that there are no places which he can get into where you can't follow, should iguana-retrieval become necessary, and you should not let him roam at all if he is too wild—cornered iguanas can injure themselves trying to fight you. Do not use liquid or powder carpet cleaners in your iguana-room— even a thorough vacuuming will leave plenty of residue behind to poison your iguana, both by inhalation and by the inevitable licking as he checks things out. Make sure, also, that there are no other household chemicals or pesticides either in use or in storage in your iguana area. All are poisonous, even the so-called "non-toxic" pesticides such as boric acid. Make sure the floor is covered in something soft, and then provide some sturdy furnishings that he can climb on. In most cases, your iguana will pick out a favorite area and will tend to spend most of his time there, particularly if you have furnished it enticingly.

If you allow your iguana to roam, avoid the tendency of many pet-owners to want all their assorted pets to appear as one big, happy peaceable kingdom. Cats, dogs, and iguanas (or any other reptiles) have little natural inclination to become buddies and, if trouble occurs, your iguana will almost certainly emerge the loser—much better to simply keep your iguana apart from other household pets to ensure his safety.

HEALTH PROBLEMS

Good healthcare for a new iguana begins with isolation, observation, and a trip to the vet. Whenever you acquire a new iguana, it should undergo a period of quarantine, especially if you have other iguanas. During the quarantine period, which should last for several weeks, your iguana should be housed by himself so that you will have the chance to catch any incipient health problems before they spread to any other reptiles which you may have. You should also use this time to make detailed observations of your new iguana, so that you will be able to spot any subtle symptoms or problems.

Your iguana should also make his first trip to the veterinarian during his quarantine period. Your vet should check his overall condition and appearance, examine him for external parasites such as mites or ticks and, most important, do a fecal examination to detect any internal parasites. In order for your vet to do a fecal exam you will, of course, need to collect and bring along a sample. The sample should be fresh—ideally less than four hours old. If your iguana is not too great at pooping on demand, as most aren't, a proper exam is still possible for up to twelve hours if the sample is placed in a well-sealed plastic bag and refrigerated. Don't submit the small amounts of yellow or whitish uric acid for fecal checks—poop looks like poop, and that's what you need to have. Your vet should perform both a fecal flotation to check

for worms and a smear to check for protozoans, so make sure that you bring a large enough sample. Just don't let your sample dry out. A sample that's dried out or more than 12 hours old isn't a sample— it's a fossil.

Many reptiles simply do not understand the physical principles of glass and will continually rub their snouts against it in the hopes of 'getting through.' Such activity usually leads to severe rostral sores and abrasions. Photo by Isabelle Francais.

Rostral Abrasions

Abrasions to the rostrum— the big nose-scale and the area surrounding it—are common among all captive reptiles, and are caused by repeated rubbing of the snout against the sides of the cage. The most common cause of this snout-rubbing behavior is the simple inability of reptiles in general to

understand the concept of glass—with no visible barrier between themselves and the outside world, they will struggle endlessly to get through the invisible glass barrier. Housing your iguana in a cage with solid or wire-mesh sides will go a long way toward ending this behavior—once your iguana understands where the walls really are, he'll usually stop battering himself against them. If you can't adapt the cage, cover the sides with towels or stick on some strips of tape—unsightly, perhaps, but much better than an iguana with a perpetually raw, abraded snout.

If adjusting the cage conditions doesn't end the snout-rubbing, your iguana may be under stress from human traffic, from the presence of other pets, or simply from the unfamiliarity of his new environment. All three of these possibilities can be easily addressed by adding a hidebox to the cage, so your iguana can get away from it all periodically.

The rostral abrasions themselves are usually superficial and easily treated. They will normally heal up on their own once the cause of the behavior is removed, but if they are deep or slow to heal you can apply a little topical antibiotic to the abrasion. Use an ointment rather than a cream, as it will stay on better and will not dissolve in your iguana's drinking water when he sticks his nose in his bowl.

Thermal Burns

Thermal burns commonly result from the use of heated rocks, but they can also occur through the use of spot lights, clear (unfrosted) light bulbs, or placement of lights and heaters inside the cage instead of outside.

Thermal burns appear as discolored, blistered, or oozing skin, with the epidermis separating from the dermis and eventually sloughing off. Burns of any type are one of the most serious insults that an animal's body can sustain, so even burns that appear minor should be evaluated by a veterinarian before you attempt to treat them. With proper veterinarian-assisted care, your iguana should recover, but the scales in the burned area may or may not regenerate, depending on the depth of the burns.

Electrocution

Electrocution can occur whenever iguanas and electricity cross paths, particularly if there is water present. Heated rocks can produce a potentially fatal shock if they are damp or cracked, as can any of your lights or heaters if they come into contact with water or are shorted out due to damage or defects. Signs of electrocution are collapse, frequently accompanied by paralysis, and occasional obvious burn or char marks.

If you come upon your iguana immediately after electrocution has occurred and you understand the basics of cardiopulmonary resuscitation, by all means give it a shot—it wouldn't be the first time that

someone has successfully resuscitated an animal, including an iguana. Adjust the cardiac compressions to suit the size of such a small body, and cover both his mouth and his nose when breathing him. Just don't breathe too hard—his lungs are tiny, and you can rupture them by overinflation. Of course, CPR should never be started on anybody (animal or human) who is still breathing on their own—if your iguana is breathing for himself, just bundle him up and get him to a vet ASAP. In any case, performing CPR on an iguana is a whole lot harder than simple prevention—keep the electricity away from the water, keep them both away from your iguana, and put ground-fault interrupters on the circuits that power your cage accessories.

Heat Prostration

Heat prostration results from too hot a cage, a cage that has no cool hiding places, and a closed cage left in direct sunlight. The symptoms are much the same as those of electrocution, minus the burn marks, and the overall appearance is of general collapse. Treatment consists of immediate removal from the heat and soaking in lukewarm water to cool him down. If he is breathing on his own, take him immediately to the vet—if he is no longer breathing, attempt CPR as for electrocution.

Broken Bones

Broken bones in iguanas can be caused by falls, by having things fall on an animal, by underlying deficiency diseases which result in weakened bones, and by the climb-

ing and jumping that is a normal part of everyday iguana life. Broken bones need the immediate attention of a veterinarian, but are treatable with proper professional care and, in most cases, will heal with few residual problems.

While breaks of the major bones are relatively uncommon, broken toes seem to be a frequent misfortune of iguana life. The broken digit will usually appear swollen in the region of the break and will be useless below the swelling. Attempting to splint a broken toe will usually result in more discomfort to the iguana than simply allowing the toe to heal on its own, which in most cases it will do without any further problems. Many older iguanas will have several floppy toes from old breaks, without any noticeable impairment of their climbing ability or any difficulties with their other activities.

While broken toes normally heal without incident, you need to watch for potential abscesses or infections. If the swelling fails to diminish, if lumps appear at the site of the break, or if there is any external drainage from the affected area, you will need to get your iguana to the vet for appropriate treatment.

Dermatitis

Dermatitis is the general term for a variety of skin disorders. Dermatitis can appear as dry patches or as oozing lesions. It can also appear as black patches which are thought to be fungal in origin, or as blisters. The variety of causative organisms is even greater than the variety of different appearances, so all cases of dermatitis really need to be assessed by a veterinarian prior to treatment.

Virtually all cases of skin disorders are direct results of poor husbandry. Blistering of the skin (when not caused by a thermal burn) is a result of a cage that is too damp, too dirty, or both. You will need to see your vet to clear up this type of blister disease, but you can clean up the cage conditions right away. The humidity within the cage should not be so great that it is always condensing and leaving puddles, and any spilled water should be mopped up right away. Instead of one constant level of humidity, mist the cage and allow it to dry out in between. And, of course, clean it up and keep it that way in the future.

In addition to the skin disorders that are directly caused by dirty cage conditions, iguanas kept in unclean cages can inoculate each other—and you—with bacteria by piercing skin with dirty claws. When an infection is introduced in this manner into a reptile, the infected site will frequently become abscessed. Abscesses in reptiles do not open up to the surface and drain on their own, and are so thoroughly walled-off that antibiotics cannot reach them. If an infection becomes abscessed, surgical excision will become necessary. If the infection from the inoculated material enters the bloodstream, it can also become disseminated throughout the body and damage other organs.

Dry Gangrene

Dry gangrene is a condition usually found in tails and toes and is caused by a lack of circulation to the affected area. It is commonly seen as a darkening of the affected part, followed eventually by the loss of the part.

Dry gangrene of the tail can be the result of injury or infection, or it can seemingly appear spontaneously. If allowed to progress, the tail will slowly fall off a section at a time. The only way to arrest dry gangrene of the tail is by surgical amputation above the affected area, so if you see it developing in your iguana, act promptly.

Dry gangrene of the toes is also treatable only by amputation, but you have a greater opportunity to deal with the causes when toes are affected. Gangrene, as well as other types of infections of the toes, is most commonly caused by constriction of the affected part. These constrictions can be caused by retention of bands of old, unshed skin or they can be caused by an accumulation of fibers, most common in iguanas that are allowed the run of the house. Free-roamers collect these fibers as they hike across carpets and upholstery, and the fibers become wrapped around the toes, cutting off circulation. It is also not unusual to find wayward hairs fallen from the heads of household members wrapped around an iguana's toes. Iguanas can also pick up fibers from various types of cage substrates, as well, so keeping your iguana confined instead of free-roaming is no guarantee that he won't pick up fibers. To keep his toes free of fibers and their potential for damage and infection, check your iguana often—use a magnifying glass, if necessary—and remove any hairs or fibers that you find.

Care of the Claws

Iguana claws grow constantly and are rarely worn down in captivity as they would be in a natural environment. Left untrimmed, overly-long claws can be broken and pulled out as your iguana climbs in his cage, and they can certainly make handling him an exercise in tolerating pain. You can trim your iguana's claws with a set of regular people-use nail clippers or you can use a hot-wire trimmer such as that used by dog groomers, although a hot-wire trimmer costs a lot more to produce a result that's very similar to that obtained with the nail clippers.

Surprisingly, most iguanas don't object much to having their claws trimmed. You should clip only the tips—clipping any deeper into the claw can nick the blood vessels. If you do nick the blood vessel, either stop the bleeding with a styptic pencil or let it stop on its own. Once it has stopped, make sure you return the 'patient' to a squeaky-clean cage so that his nicked claw won't become infected from cage crud while it heals. Also, if your iguana decides that he's had enough before you've trimmed all his claws, just let him go and finish up another time—wrestling matches involving iguanas, claws, and sharp instruments are virtually guaranteed to leave somebody injured.

Breakage of Tail

Your iguana's tail won't fall off in your hand, but it can be broken by rough handling, as well as by a fall or by objects falling on him. A freshly broken tail requires veterinary attention to prevent infection from taking hold at the wound site. Properly tended, and protected from further damage, the tail will heal and, to a limited extent, regenerate. This regrowth can take a year or more, and the smaller, regenerated portion of the tail will lack any further regenerative capabilities should it be broken again. There is also extensive evidence that the loss of a portion of the tail compromises the overall health of the animal. In lizards the tail functions as a warehouse for the stored fat and nutrients upon which the lizard can draw in times of stress, and the lack of this backup system will cause difficulties in egg production in females, and shortened lifespans in both sexes.

Anemia

Anemia is usually secondary to another underlying health problem such as intestinal or blood-borne parasites or malabsorption of nutrients. Anemia appears as pale mouth and gum tissue and will leave your iguana susceptible to other diseases if the underlying cause is not corrected. If your iguana exhibits symptoms of anemia, a fecal exam and a blood test will be necessary to determine the root cause of the problem.

External Parasites

Mites and/or ticks are common on wild-caught iguanas, but can also appear on captive-bred ones as a result of the crowded conditions during shipping. Mites

appear as tiny black dots moving about mostly at night, and hiding during the day beneath the scales. Mites almost always occur in large colonies, numbering in the hundreds and even thousands in very bad cases.

Ticks are a little easier to spot, since they usually occur singly or in small groups, and grow very large. Even small ticks will show eventually— they will attach themselves and suck so much blood that their bodies will bloat and make them conspicuous. Ticks often find a home on the soft tissue posterior to the vent, but they can appear anywhere.

Mites will not infest you, as they are the wrong kind to be interested in mammals, but they can spread like wildfire throughout a reptile collection, transmitting diseases at each stop. To eradicate mites, treat with a topical ointment as prescribed by your vet. Some veterinary medications commonly used for elimination of internal parasites in mammals work just dandy for external application in reptiles. Let your vet direct you as to dosages and application methods, etc.

Some keepers use small pieces of pest strip kept in a plastic container that has tiny holes drilled through the lid and sides. The idea is to place the container in the iguana's cage and leave it there for about five days. As long as the iguana can't get to the strip (in which case he probably will eat it and very quickly die), this method works fairly well. All water should be removed from the cage during the time of treatment because the strip has a tainting effect on it.

Either way, the point is, an

untreated case of mites can spread quickly throughout a reptile collection, so treat at the first sign of a problem. Even a completely clean collection can become infested if one of its members is exposed during a trip to the vet's or while being boarded during vacations. If you must board your iguana, you will be much better off doing it at the vet—a veterinarian's boarding facilities are no guarantee that your iguana won't pick up something, but the chances are immeasurably greater that he will be infected with something if you board him at a pet shop. In any case, make sure that he will be boarded in private quarters, not housed with a group of other animals.

Ticks, unlike mites, are completely unconcerned with whose blood they suck, and a tick removed and left alive will be just as happy to bite you as he was to bite your iguana. Ticks also transmit a variety of diseases ranging from the merely unpleasant to the potentially lethal, so check for them carefully and get rid of them properly. Ticks can be removed by extracting them with a pair of tweezers, making sure that the tweezer tips are clutching the tick as close to the iguana's skin as possible where the tick is attached. If you break off only the tick's body but the head remains, severe infections could result.

You can also try covering the tick with petroleum jelly, cutting off the tick's oxygen supply and either killing it outright or at least urging it to release itself. Once a tick has been removed, swab the infected area with hydrogen peroxide once a day for at least three days and watch the animal carefully for any signs of local infection at the site or of internal infection.

Internal Parasites

All wild (and wild-caught) animals carry a certain parasite load, and in most cases will cause the animal no real harm, since killing one's host is a poor strategy for a parasite to adopt. These parasites normally don't become a noticeable problem until the animal is weakened by the stress of captivity, or by poor general husbandry. As more captive-bred, farm-raised iguanas become available, the once-common parasite problems of wild-caught iguanas are becoming more infrequent—yet another good reason to purchase captive-bred animals. Even if your iguana has been farm-raised, however, he should still have the blood and fecal checks done, as any parasites constitute an unnecessary drain on his health and resources.

The most common parasites are the roundworms and tape worms which make their home in the gastrointestinal tract, but malaria, trypanosomes, and filariae in the blood or flukes in the liver and gallbladder may also be present. Symptoms of gastrointestinal parasites can include blood in the droppings, a peculiar smell or appearance, or the presence of visible segments in the case of tapeworms. Blood-borne parasites may announce their presence by producing anemia, as previously mentioned, and either type of parasite can result in poor appetite or appearance, and in general restlessness.

Treatment for any type of parasite begins with appropriate exams at the vet's. There is really no one antiparasitical drug that will treat a broad spectrum of parasites—treatment is quite specific and requires precise identification of the organism. It is also important that your vet treat your iguana with drugs that have been proven safe in reptiles, as those that are intended for use in dogs and cats can be harmful or lethal when used in reptiles.

If your iguana has the symptoms or appearance of an animal with parasites but his fecal check shows no evidence of their presence, wait a bit and do another one. Parasites, their segments, or their eggs may not always be shed continuously, so symptoms that persist despite a negative result on the first exam will require a second one.

Bloating

Bloating, also known as tympany, looks pretty much like it sounds—the iguana appears swollen, sometimes extremely so, throughout its abdominal area. Bloating can result from feeding too much fermentable sugary food, or from a change from a high-fiber diet to sugar-containing foods. Bloating can also be caused by food that has become impacted in the intestinal tract, or food that has rotted within the gut due to lack of heat.

The appearance of bloating is obvious due to the gross distortion of the iguana's body, and is potentially lethal due to the severe pressure it exerts on the heart, lungs, and other internal organs. Your veterinarian can administer gas-lysing agents which will break up the gas pockets, and drugs to stimulate intestinal motility. The best things for you to do yourself are to give warm baths during the course of treatment, and to spot the symptoms in time for treatment to be effective.

Diarrhea

Normal iguana droppings have a large watery component, but the main portion of the stool should be somewhat firm. Diarrhea is a common symptom of intestinal parasites, so you should check for their presence. Diarrhea can also result from feeding watery foods such as melons, a condition which can be treated by a simple change of diet and by adding some softened alfalfa pellets for bulk to your iguana's meal.

If the diarrhea persists for any length of time, your iguana can become rapidly dehydrated. Your vet will need to support the treatment of protracted diarrhea by rehydration through injection, and if vomiting is also present an immediate trip to the vet is indicated. Throughout the course of treatment you can assist your iguana by administering an electrolyte-replacement solution of some kind or another.

Constipation

Constipation can be caused by inappropriate diet, lack of sufficient heat, lack of water, use of improper cage substrates leading to ingestion, or by the presence of parasites. Another cause of constipation, particularly in free-roaming iguanas, is assorted dust, gunk, and household fibers.

Due to their tendency to check out everything by sticking their tongues on it, iguanas can pick up enormous amounts of fibrous grunge which can consolidate within their intestines. Veterinary laxatives will usually fix this problem in short order—just make sure to use a laxative obtained from your veterinarian and not one intended for human use.

Whatever the cause turns out to be, treat it right away. Make sure there is ample water available, get rid of cage substrates that can be ingested, chop food into smaller, more digestible particles, raise the temperature, treat with laxatives—whatever is necessary. Just don't waste time getting started—untreated constipation will get worse and worse as more water is reabsorbed within the intestine, the feces get drier, and the impaction progresses to the point that surgery becomes necessary.

In cases of either diarrhea or constipation, you won't know something is abnormal unless you're familiar with what's normal for your iguana. In general, iguanas will defecate once or twice daily but, as with all creatures, that can vary from individual to individual. Just make sure that the droppings are normal in appearance and that the frequency is within the normal range for your animal.

Prolapse of Internal Organs

A prolapsed organ is one which has slipped out of its proper place, and it is possible for a prolapsed organ to pop out through your iguana's vent. Rectal mucous membrane, loops of intestine, and one or both hemipenes in males can

suddenly protrude, and this is a condition that is every bit as serious as it looks.

Spontaneous prolapses do occur, but more often the cause is straining due to constipation, or imbalances in ion equilibrium due to vitamin and mineral deficiencies which result in over-relaxation of the muscular tissue. If this occurs in your reptile, fix his diet later but get the mechanical difficulties seen to immediately. These are internal organs that are hanging out and they can become damaged or seriously infected from exposure to the exterior, or they can become strangulated—that is, the blood supply can be cut off in the prolapsed area resulting in tissue necrosis and loss of the affected part. Treatment requires prompt action by a veterinarian—occasionally the prolapsed part can be cleaned up and massaged back into place, but surgical intervention is frequently required.

Metabolic Bone Disease and Calcium/Phosphorus Imbalances

Calcium and phosphorus are critical dietary elements for all reptiles, most especially for iguanas, but even more important than the elements themselves are the proportions in which they are given, and an imbalance between the two is the most frequently-seen deficiency problem in iguanas. The minimum ratio is 1:1 calcium to phosphorus—that is, equal parts of each substance—and the optimum ratio is at least 2:1, or twice as much calcium as phosphorus. Deficiencies are regrettably common, with the prime offenders being a diet too rich in animal protein, or contain-

ing too much lettuce. This type of deficiency disease affects the same structures and systems that are damaged by lack of full-spectrum light, so iguanas that don't receive enough full-spectrum radiation (which is most of them in captivity) can decline even more rapidly as the two conditions compound each other.

The mechanism by which calcium/phosphorus imbalances arise is a complex one, and involves a cascade of metabolic events. The trigger can be either a lack of calcium, or the presence of too much phosphorus, which depletes calcium stores even in the presence of adequate dietary calcium. When serum calcium levels reach the minimum threshold level, hormones from the parathyroid glands initiate reabsorption of calcium from the iguana's bones. These hormones also cause the kidneys to begin off-loading as much phosphorus as possible in an attempt to eliminate the problem, and they stimulate the conversion of vitamin D to its biologically active form. It is the active D which regulates calcium absorption from either dietary sources or bone matrix.

This form of metabolic bone disease can also be caused by kidney dysfunction—the kidneys in their diseased condition anomalously begin dumping calcium and retaining phosphorus. As the serum phosphorus level rises, the parathyroids again begin secreting hormones to pull calcium out of the bones, but in this case they are at war with the activity of the diseased kidneys, and the whole process can escalate out of control in a very short time, producing very rapid bone loss. Because this condition is caused by an underlying and severe kidney dysfunction, it is usually fatal, whereas the standard dietary-induced difficulties are somewhat easier to treat. A calcium/phosphorus imbalance shows itself in the loss of mineralization in the bones with resulting skeletal deformities and pathological (spontaneous) fractures. In general, the bones of an iguana suffering from calcium/phosphorus imbalance are poorly ossified—they lack the hard, distinct formations typical of healthy bone tissue. This type of nutritional illness can be easily diagnosed by X-ray—the bones will appear fuzzy and indistinct, with noticeable deviation from the straight lines of healthy bone, and will have a spongy appearance. In addition, the outer bone will appear thicker, this thickening being an attempt to shore up the weakening bone structure. When bone is demineralized, it can no longer withstand the pull of its attached muscles, which results in curvature and shortening of the jaws from the pull exerted by the tongue muscles. Visual diagnosis can also be made when swelling of the hindlimbs or fine muscle tremors are observed.

The progression of this metabolic bone disease, or osteodystrophy, can be very deceptive in iguanas. All lizards can be affected by these nutritional deficiencies, but iguanas are particularly susceptible, and the appearance can easily go unnoticed until the lizard is very sick. Due to the swelling produced in the limbs and tail, an affected iguana looks at first glance to be a fat, well-fed specimen, but if the diet has consisted of lettuce and fruit, calcium/phosphorus deficiency should be suspected right away.

In general, the treatment for the diseases of calcium/phosphorus imbalance requires injections of calcium gluconate or calcium lactate several times weekly, orally-administered calcium, vitamin D supplements and, of course, an improvement in the iguana's diet. Iguanas recovering from metabolic bone disease should be given finely pureed foods, or baby food if you don't have a food processor, as jaw movement will be too painful for them to do much chewing. Your iguana will also be in severe joint and muscle pain, so avoid any unnecessary handling until his treatment is complete.

Rickets

Rickets is another bone disease that has its roots in the metabolic processes, and while the end result is the same as metabolic bone disease, the pathway by which it occurs is quite different. The bone deformities characteristic of rickets occur when there is sufficient calcium present, but there is not enough vitamin D available, either from nutritional sources or from full-spectrum light. Without an adequate supply of vitamin D, whatever calcium may be present cannot be absorbed. Without improvement in both dietary and full-spectrum sources of vitamin D, the skeletal deformities of rickets will be the result.

Thiamine (B₁) Deficiency

Thiamine (B_1) deficiency is usually not the result of a dietary insufficiency. Reptiles most often become thiamine-deficient from eating a diet containing too much frozen food, which contains thiaminase. This enzyme destroys the thiamine obtained from other dietary sources, and from the normally adequate supply synthesized by the intestinal flora and absorbed from the digestive tract. Thiamine deficiency can also result from lengthy antibiotic therapy, which destroys the intestinal bacteria responsible for thiamine synthesis.

Thiamine deficiency produces disorders of the central nervous system and cardiac problems. The neurological problems associated with this central nervous system dysfunction result in unusual behavior and posture, loss of appetite, muscle tremors, blindness and, if untreated, death.

The best treatment is prevention—don't feed frozen vegetables. If you're absolutely out of everything else, you can get away with it once in a while, but you should counteract its ill effects by slipping a B_1 tablet in with the meal—25mg/kg is about right, but dosage is not critical. If the deficiency has progressed substantially, injectable thiamine HCl should be given, along with a correction in diet. If the thiamine deficiency has occurred due to antibiotic therapy, your iguana can be reinoculated with the appropriate microbes. Cultures for reinoculation are available through your veterinarian, who can best advise you on their use and administration.

Vitamin A Deficiency

In general, vitamin A deficiencies occur in herbivores who are receiving a carotene-poor diet. Newly-hatched specimens get their first dose of vitamin A from the yolk around which they develop, and they store enough of it in their livers to get them off to a good start. These reserves will deplete quickly, however, if dietary sources are not provided, and a high-protein diet will speed up the depletion process. Epithelial tissue—the tissue that forms a sheet covering a body surface or lining a body cavity—begins to deteriorate rapidly, resistance to disease begins to decline, and if these reserves are not replaced, eye and respiratory infections are the usual result.

Symptoms will appear as swelling of the eyelids, gaping of the mouth, wheezing, and a runny nose. To treat the secondary symptoms, rinse the eyes with sterile saline solution to remove any discharge or crusty material. Applying a topical opthalmic ointment will provide some relief in the form of lubrication, as well as make some superficial progress against the infection, but to eradicate these infections a course of systemic antibiotic therapy should also be instituted. To treat the underlying cause—the vitamin deficiency—administer vitamin A. If your creature is eating, break open a vitamin A capsule and administer the contents orally by putting it on his food. In most instances, however, the animal will have stopped eating, so injectable A must be given. Improvement in the diet is also a must.

Too much vitamin A can also cause problems. A diet containing too much A usually results from feeding cat and dog food, or by the overly-enthusiastic use of vitamin supplements. Overdoses of vitamin A are often given in an attempt to stimulate appetite, although there is no evidence that it is effective for this purpose. Symptoms will appear as dry, flaky skin followed by loss of skin tissue and infection of the now-exposed underlying tissues. Fluid-filled blisters will also form on the skin, and will shortly slough. The fluid loss from this process can be severe, but most will recover if treated promptly.

Treatment consists of antibiotics to counteract secondary infections of the raw tissues, and an abrupt halt to the vitamin overdoses. Overdose problems are usually the result of overuse of injectables, and in any case it is highly uncommon to encounter a deficiency of vitamin A in herbivores—if you really feel a burning need for vitamin A supplements, give oral A in its natural forms such as carrots, corn, squash, and greens.

Vitamin C Deficiency

Vitamin C deficiencies are found in all types of reptiles and, as with vitamin A deficiency, produce or at least contribute to secondary disorders. Early symptoms are vague, consisting mostly of depressed immune function and decreased resistance to other diseases, and a lack of vitamin C also appears to play a role in infectious stomatitis, or mouth rot. As the deficiency progresses, bleeding from the gums may be seen and, in severe cases, spontaneous rupture of the skin can also occur.

Treatment consists of giving therapeutic vitamin C, along with antibiotics, to creatures with mouth rot, and thereafter providing better dietary sources. Any animal with other secondary infections should also receive additional C. For vegetarians, simply increase the amount of C-rich fruits and vegetables, and a vitamin supplement for preventive purposes should become a regular part of the diet. By way of encouragement, a vitamin C deficiency usually responds quite rapidly to treatment.

Vitamin E Deficiency

Deficiencies of vitamin E result in a type of muscular dystrophy—muscle fibers swell, eventually becoming atrophied and replaced with fibrous connective tissue. The initial appearance of vitamin E deficiency can be similar enough to calcium deficiency that serum calcium should always be checked prior to treatment. Lack of E usually occurs from the feeding of an unnatural or inappropriate diet and—as always—repairing the diet is the first and most important step. It has also been shown that some type of relationship exists between the utilization of dietary E and selenium (although the nature of the relationship is unclear) and iguanas who are fed items grown in selenium-poor soils are at greater risk of developing vitamin E deficiencies.

Vitamin K Deficiency

Deficiencies of vitamin K are rare, but do occasionally occur. Vitamin K is necessary for proper clotting of blood, and deficiencies have occasionally resulted from ingestion of food contaminated with the anticoagulant coumadin and its derivatives, which are common rodenticides. If this type of poisoning can be ruled out, the most likely source of the problem is destruction of the intestinal flora (where vitamin K is synthesized) due to prolonged antibiotic therapy.

A deficiency of K will often appear initially as bleeding of the gums without evidence of other problems such as mouth rot, or by other spontaneous bleeding. This deficiency responds rapidly to injections of vitamin K, but its administration is best left to your veterinarian—vitamin K is required in extremely minute quantities and too large a dose can have serious consequences for your reptile. In addition, if antibiotic therapy appears to be the culprit, reinoculation of the proper intestinal microbes is indicated.

Iodine

Deficiencies of iodine can be caused either by a lack of dietary iodine, or by feeding foods that induce iodine deficiency. The major offenders are brussels sprouts, cabbage, kale, broccoli, soybean sprouts and cauliflower and are best avoided, but if you feed these things you must supplement the diet with additional iodine. Iodine solutions are available but taste so bad that no reptile in his right mind will take them, and they have a relatively high potential for toxicity if administered incorrectly. The best way to supplement an iodine-poor diet is through the use of kelp tablets several times a week.

Nutritionally-induced thyroid disease is closely related to iodine deficiency, although it can also be caused by the drinking of very hard tap water. The symptoms are difficult to diagnose, but if left untreated this thyroid dysfunction will result in lethargy, refusal of food and loss of muscle tissue. Treatment consists of a change in diet, and the addition of 1 milliliter of .2% potassium iodide solution per liter of drinking water, if your veterinarian recommends it and you can get your iguana to take it.

Trace Minerals

Deficiencies of trace minerals are most commonly diagnosed in iguanas who are fed only a limited number of fruit and vegetable types, but it is not a particularly useful diagnosis as little is really known about just what and how much of the elements are needed. In iguanas—and in everybody else—the best protection is simply a well-rounded diet.

Vitamins and minerals are as necessary to reptiles as they are to us and deficiency diseases can hit them a lot harder and faster, as they are wholly dependent on us for their diet and don't always get what they really need. In addition, juveniles are the first to be affected due to their heightened nutritional requirements, and a deficiency during formative stages can leave an iguana affected for a lifetime. For general preventive maintenance nothing beats a diet with the most variety possible, and a sharp eye for anything out of the ordinary.

Visceral Gout and Renal Disorders

Visceral gout and kidney disorders are also common nutritional diseases of captive reptiles. These are diseases of uric-acid clearance—that is, the reptile loses the ability to rid its body of nitrogenous waste products. Excessive amounts of protein, the feeding of organ meats such as liver, use of nephrotoxic drugs, too high a temperature, too little humidity and inadequate water intake create a complex of diseases, all of which can exacerbate each other if they occur simultaneously. Iguanas are very efficient at processing plant material, but animal protein and the large amount of urates that its metabolism produces quickly overwhelm their urate-clearance abilities. When a reptile's metabolism is overloaded with protein, his kidneys can't keep up with the load. This inability to process and excrete the uric acid results in its building up within the body. The uric acid is then deposited in the joints, which is the standard form of gout, and in the visceral organs, which is known as visceral gout. These deposits can appear within the heart, liver, and kidneys as well as other, more disseminated sites, and bladder stones may also occur. When an iguana is suffering from an inability to eliminate uric acid from his body, he will generally refuse to feed, become lethargic, and have difficulty in moving and shedding his skin. Sometimes swollen joints will be visible, but the absence of this swelling does not rule out gout.

Diagnosis, if it is to be anything other than postmortem, should be prompt. The disease will reveal itself by X-ray, as the deposits produced by gout in both the viscera and the joints are opaque to X-radiation, and will show up as white masses in unlikely places. If the results of the X-ray are inconclusive, positive identification can be made by microscope under polarized light, either at necropsy or by needle biopsy in a living reptile. Polarized light is light which is vibrating in one plane only, instead of the random vibrations of ordinary light, and this peculiarity makes certain features, particularly in crystals, more apparent. In this case, polarized light shows the uric acid crystals in clear relief. If the animal has died, it is no problem to obtain a large enough sample for easy examination, but if you've caught the problem prior to its being fatal, examination of urate deposits will have to be done by needle biopsy, wherein a needle is inserted into the deposit and a small amount aspirated for examination.

Treatment consists of a better diet—that is, one with more variety—and support with injections of vitamins, physiological saline, and glucose once a week for about three weeks. Iguanas should get a better assortment of vegetables, with as many fresh ones as possible.

Lack of water, either from a lowered intake on the part of the iguana, or by failure to provide him with an adequate supply, can also produce these disorders. Antibiotic therapy which causes disturbances of uric-acid clearance also requires plentiful water—if your iguana requires antibiotics, monitor his water intake

carefully. If he is reluctant to drink, you may need to have your veterinarian administer replacement fluids by injection.

Respiratory Infections

Respiratory infections often result from drafty or chilly cages, particularly when combined with the stress of shipping, handling, or dirty and unpleasant cage conditions. Respiratory distress is indicated by abnormal sounds from the lungs, fluid bubbling out from the nose or mouth, rapid breathing, loss of appetite, dark color, and occasionally by open-mouthed coughing. If any of these signs are present, prompt veterinary attention is required.

Respiratory infections are particularly hard on reptiles in general, including iguanas, as reptiles have no diaphragm. Without this strong sheet of muscle beneath their lungs, reptiles can cough but they can't really do it very efficiently. This inability to give a good, muscular cough makes it much more difficult to expel fluids and infectious material from the lungs, and makes it considerably harder for reptiles to keep their lungs clear while throwing off the infection.

Left untreated, respiratory infections progress in only one direction—downhill. Treatment of a respiratory infection requires fast, aggressive antibiotic therapy if the animal is to recover, so get to a vet right away at the first signs of respiratory distress.

Occasionally, symptoms of respiratory distress may be caused by certain types of parasites which pass through the oral cavity and lungs on their way to their preferred

sites in the gastrointestinal tract. To rule out parasites as the cause of the distress, your vet should perform an oropharyngeal smear—a swab of the mouth and throat—to check for the presence of parasites.

Zoonotic Infection

Periodically a rash of stories go around about people who have contracted *Salmonella* from their iguanas. While it is undeniably true that *Salmonella* can be passed from iguana to human, it is important to remember that not only can you catch worse stuff from the family dog, but it is also estimated that up to 80% of our domestic egg and poultry supply is contaminated with *Salmonella* bacteria. In short, *Salmonella* is everywhere all the time anyway, and protecting yourself from infection is simply a matter of using your head, washing your hands, and keeping a nail brush on every sink so you can get rid of whatever gunk gets trapped beneath your fingernails. When you handle your iguana, or any animal, wash up—and require that other family members do the same.

If your iguana needs treatment, take him to the vet and obtain your medications there. There are many over-the-counter medications sold that purport to treat everything from loss of appetite to intestinal parasites, but you can rest assured that if it's strong enough to actually work, you won't find it available over the counter. The one exception is topical antibiotic ointments. Other than that, if your iguana is sick get real medicine, and get it from your veterinarian.

knowledgment

s volume in the *Basic Domestic Pet Library* series was researched in part at the tario Veterinary college at the University of Guelph in Guelph, Ontario, and was blished under the auspice of Dr. Herbert R. Axelrod.

A world-renown scientist, explorer, author, university professor, lecturer, and blisher, Dr. Axelrod is the best-known tropical fish expert in the world and the inder and chairman of T.F.H. Publications, Inc., the largest and most respected blisher of pet literature in the world. He has written 16 definitive texts on Ichthyology cluding the bestselling *Handbook of Tropical Aquarium Fishes)*, published more than books on individual species of fish for the hobbyist, written hundreds of articles, d discovered hundreds of previously unknown species, six of which have been named er him.

)r. Axelrod holds a Ph.D and was awarded an Honorary Doctor of Science degree by : University of Guelph, where he is now an adjunct professor in the Department of ology. He has served on the American Pet Products Manufacturers Association ard of Governors and is a member of the American Society of Herpetologists and thyologists, the Biometric Society, the New York Zoological Society, the New York ademy of Sciences, the American Fisheries Society, the National Research Council, : National Academy of Sciences, and numerous aquarium societies around the world. n 1977, Dr. Axelrod was awarded the Smithson Silver Medal for his ichthyological d charitable endeavors by the Smithsonian Institution. A decade later, he was elected endowment member of the American Museum of Natural History and was named a : member of the James Smithson Society by the Smithsonian Associates' national ard. He has donated in excess of $50 million in recent years to the American Museum National History, the University of Guelph, and other institutions.

INDEX

Bathing, 46
Features of body, 11
    claws, 15
    parietal eye, 12
    salt glands, 12
    shedding, 11
Feeding, 36
    planning a diet, 36
    water, 42
    what to feed, 39
Free-Range Iguanas, 53
Handling and taming, 52
Health problems, 55
    anemia, 58
    breakage of tail, 57
    bloating, 59
    broken bones, 56
    claws, 57
    constipation, 59
    dermatitis, 56
    diarrhea, 59
    dry gangrene, 57
    electrocution, 56
    external parasites, 58
    heat prostration, 56
    internal parasites, 59
    iodine, 63
    metabolic bone disease, 60
    prolapse of internal organs, 60
    respiratory infections, 64
    rickets, 61
    rostral abrasions, 55
    thermal burns, 56
    Thiamine (B) Deficiency, 61
    trace minerals, 63
    Vitamin A Deficiency, 62
    Vitamin C Deficiency, 62
    Vitamin E Deficiency, 62
    Vitamin K Deficiency, 62
    Zoonotic infection, 64
Heat, 20
    heated rocks, 26
Housing, 16
    cages, 16
    cleaning, 32
    electrical engineering, 33
    furnishings, 16
    screen tops, 18
    substrate, 32
Light, 28
    full-spectrum, 28
    regular, 28
Reproduction, 47
Selection process, 6